I0412166

EXAMINING TSA'S MANAGEMENT OF THE SCREENING PARTNERSHIP PROGRAM

HEARING

BEFORE THE

SUBCOMMITTEE ON TRANSPORTATION SECURITY

OF THE

COMMITTEE ON HOMELAND SECURITY HOUSE OF REPRESENTATIVES

ONE HUNDRED THIRTEENTH CONGRESS

SECOND SESSION

JULY 29, 2014

Serial No. 113-81

Printed for the use of the Committee on Homeland Security

Available via the World Wide Web: http://www.gpo.gov/fdsys/

U.S. GOVERNMENT PUBLISHING OFFICE

92-898 PDF WASHINGTON : 2015

For sale by the Superintendent of Documents, U.S. Government Publishing Office
Internet: bookstore.gpo.gov Phone: toll free (866) 512-1800; DC area (202) 512-1800
Fax: (202) 512-2104 Mail: Stop IDCC, Washington, DC 20402-0001

COMMITTEE ON HOMELAND SECURITY

MICHAEL T. McCAUL, Texas, *Chairman*

LAMAR SMITH, Texas
PETER T. KING, New York
MIKE ROGERS, Alabama
PAUL C. BROUN, Georgia
CANDICE S. MILLER, Michigan, *Vice Chair*
PATRICK MEEHAN, Pennsylvania
JEFF DUNCAN, South Carolina
TOM MARINO, Pennsylvania
JASON CHAFFETZ, Utah
STEVEN M. PALAZZO, Mississippi
LOU BARLETTA, Pennsylvania
RICHARD HUDSON, North Carolina
STEVE DAINES, Montana
SUSAN W. BROOKS, Indiana
SCOTT PERRY, Pennsylvania
MARK SANFORD, South Carolina
CURTIS CLAWSON, Florida

BENNIE G. THOMPSON, Mississippi
LORETTA SANCHEZ, California
SHEILA JACKSON LEE, Texas
YVETTE D. CLARKE, New York
BRIAN HIGGINS, New York
CEDRIC L. RICHMOND, Louisiana
WILLIAM R. KEATING, Massachusetts
RON BARBER, Arizona
DONDALD M. PAYNE, JR., New Jersey
BETO O'ROURKE, Texas
FILEMON VELA, Texas
ERIC SWALWELL, California
VACANCY
VACANCY

BRENDAN P. SHIELDS, *Staff Director*
JOAN O'HARA, *Acting Chief Counsel*
MICHAEL S. TWINCHEK, *Chief Clerk*
I. LANIER AVANT, *Minority Staff Director*

———

SUBCOMMITTEE ON TRANSPORTATION SECURITY

RICHARD HUDSON, North Carolina, *Chairman*

MIKE ROGERS, Alabama, *Vice Chair*
CANDICE S. MILLER, Michigan
SUSAN W. BROOKS, Indiana
MARK SANFORD, South Carolina
MICHAEL T. McCAUL, Texas *(ex officio)*

CEDRIC L. RICHMOND, Louisiana
SHEILA JACKSON LEE, Texas
ERIC SWALWELL, California
BENNIE G. THOMPSON, Mississippi *(ex officio)*

AMANDA PARIKH, *Subcommittee Staff Director*
DENNIS TERRY, *Subcommittee Clerk*
BRIAN TURBYFILL, *Minority Subcommittee Staff Director*

(II)

CONTENTS

IV

FOR THE RECORD

EXAMINING TSA'S MANAGEMENT OF THE SCREENING PARTNERSHIP PROGRAM

Tuesday, July 29, 2014

U.S. HOUSE OF REPRESENTATIVES,
SUBCOMMITTEE ON TRANSPORTATION SECURITY,
COMMITTEE ON HOMELAND SECURITY,
Washington, DC.

The subcommittee met, pursuant to call, at 9:30 a.m., in Room 311, Cannon House Office Building, Hon. Richard Hudson [Chairman of the subcommittee] presiding.

Present: Representatives Hudson, Rogers, Miller, Brooks, Sanford, McCaul, Jackson Lee, Thompson, and Swalwell.

Also present: Representative Daines.

Mr. HUDSON. The Committee on Homeland Security, Subcommittee on Transportation Security, will come to order.

The subcommittee is meeting today to hear testimony on TSA's management of the Screening Partnership Program. I recognize myself for an opening statement.

I would like to thank our witnesses for their participation in this hearing. We know your time is valuable, and we appreciate you taking the time to be here with us today.

The long-term success of TSA's Screening Partnership Program is a priority for many Members of Congress and stakeholders around the country who understand the private sector is highly capable of providing efficient and effective screening services.

Unfortunately, TSA's actions over the last few years seem to demonstrate that it does not share this goal. This hearing is an opportunity to examine the problems and current—that currently exist with the program and encourage TSA to take steps to enable more airports to choose private-sector screening.

To be clear, this does not mean airports that participate in SPP are opting out of robust Federal oversight and regulations, which were severely lacking before 9/11. It means opting to use qualified private vendors to carry out day-to-day screening functions, which lets TSA concentrate on setting and enforcing security standards.

Eighteen domestic airports currently participate in SPP. The law requires that contract screeners meet the same qualifications and receive commensurate pay and benefits to their Federal counterparts. SPP is a voluntary program, and airports must apply to participate.

Under the FAA Modernization and Reform Act of 2012, unless an airport's participation in SPP would hurt security or drive up costs, TSA must approve all new applications. This 2012 provision revived an otherwise lifeless SPP application process after the TSA administrator announced he would not expand the program unless there was a clear and substantive advantage to do so.

While I have great respect for Administrator Pistole, as far as I am concerned, there will always be at least three clear and substantial advantages to privatized screening.

No. 1, the private sector operates more efficiently than the Federal Government and can save precious taxpayer dollars.

No. 2, the private sector provides better consumer service, which is severely lacking in many of our Nation's screening checkpoints.

No. 3, while private screening—or with the private screening, TSA can stop dealing with the time-consuming human resources issues that come with managing a workforce of over 50,000 screeners.

This is not to imply that TSA has not made progress over the last few years. Under Mr. Pistole's leadership, TSA is becoming more risk-based and efficient through programs like TSA PreCheck. However, PreCheck operates just as well at SPP airports, including San Francisco International Airport, one of the largest and busiest airports in the country.

There is no reason why SPP cannot be expanded to create even greater efficiencies under a risk-based system. In order to move forward with additional SPP airports in a constructive manner, several concerns need to be addressed in the near term.

First, TSA has established a methodology for calculating Federal cost estimates for each new SPP contract based on requirements in the FAA Modernization Act, but that methodology does not include Federal retirement benefits, which we know to be a huge cost burden.

TSA is also using the average screener's salary for its FCEs, but is allowing vendors to bid the minimum screener salaries, which may be unsustainable and cause significant issues in the long term.

Second, TSA's Screening Partnership Program office does not conduct the level of outreach to airport operators as it should. To that end, TSA must make immediate changes that would include educating new airports on the benefits of SPP, communicating early and often with airports that are transitioning to SPP, and consulting the airport directors at existing SPP airports when selecting vendors for initial awards and contract recompetes.

These are simple, but crucial, changes, and the only barrier to action is TSA's well-known resistance to expanding SPP. I look forward to discussing these and many other issues with our witnesses today to ensure the program is working and prepared to expand to additional airports.

[The statement of Chairman Hudson follows:]

STATEMENT OF CHAIRMAN RICHARD HUDSON

JULY 29, 2014

I would like to thank our witnesses for their participation in this hearing. We know your time is valuable and we appreciate you taking the time to be here today.

The long-term success of TSA's Screening Partnership Program (SPP) is a priority for many Members of Congress and stakeholders around the country who understand the private sector is highly capable of providing efficient and effective screening services. Unfortunately, TSA's actions over the last few years seem to demonstrate that it does not share this goal. This hearing is an opportunity to examine the problems that currently exist within the program and encourage TSA to take steps to enable more airports to choose private-sector screening.

To be clear, this does not mean airports that participate in SPP are opting-out of robust Federal oversight and regulations, which were severely lacking before 9/11. It means opting to use qualified private vendors to carry out day-to-day screening functions, which lets TSA concentrate on setting and enforcing security standards.

Eighteen domestic airports currently participate in SPP. The law requires that contract screeners meet the same qualifications and receive commensurate pay and benefits to their Federal counterparts. SPP is a voluntary program, and airports must apply to participate. Under the FAA Modernization and Reform Act of 2012, unless an airport's participation in SPP would hurt security or drive up costs, TSA must approve all new applications.

This 2012 provision revived an otherwise lifeless SPP application process after the TSA administrator announced he would not expand the program unless there was a clear and substantial advantage to do so.

While I have great respect for Administrator Pistole, as far as I am concerned, there will always be at least three clear and substantial advantages to privatized screening:

1. The private sector operates more efficiently than the Federal Government and can save precious taxpayer dollars,

2. The private sector provides better customer service, which is severely lacking at many of our Nation's screening checkpoints, and

3. With private screening, TSA can stop dealing with the time-consuming human resources issues that come with managing a workforce of over 50,000 screeners.

This is not to imply that TSA has not made any progress over the last few years. Under Mr. Pistole's leadership, TSA is becoming more risk-based and efficient through programs like TSA PreCheck. However, PreCheck operates just as well at SPP airports, including San Francisco International Airport, one of the largest and busiest airports in the country. There is no reason why SPP cannot be expanded to create even greater efficiencies under a risk-based system.

In order to move forward with additional SPP airports in a constructive manner, several concerns needs to be addressed in the near term:

First, TSA has established a methodology for calculating Federal Cost Estimates (FCEs) for each new SPP contract based on requirements in the FAA Modernization Act, but that methodology does not include Federal retirement benefits, which we know to be a huge cost burden. TSA is also using the average screener salary for its FCEs, but is allowing vendors to bid the minimum screener salaries, which may be unsustainable and cause significant issues in the long term.

Second, TSA's Screening Partnership Program Office does not conduct the level of outreach to airport operators that it should. To that end, TSA must make immediate changes that include:

- Educating new airports on the benefits of SPP;
- Communicating early and often with airports that are transitioning to SPP;
- Consulting airport directors at existing SPP airports when selecting vendors for initial awards and contract re-competes.

These are simple but crucial changes, and the only barrier to action is TSA's well-known resistance to expanding SPP. I look forward to discussing these and many other issues with our witnesses today to ensure the program is working and prepared to expand to additional airports.

Mr. HUDSON. At this point I would ask unanimous consent that Mr. Daines, the gentleman from Montana, be permitted to participate in today's hearing. Without objection, so ordered.

Our Ranking Member, the gentleman from Louisiana, Mr. Richmond, is on his way, and I will recognize him for his statement when he arrives.

In the mean time, I would first like to yield to the gentleman from Montana, Mr. Daines, to introduce our first witness today.

Mr. DAINES. Thank you, Mr. Chairman. Thank you for hosting this important hearing this morning. It is with great pleasure that I get to sit in on this hearing and introduce a fellow Montanan.

Cindi Martin is the director of Glacier Park International Airport. With nearly 30 years of experience in aviation, she has been a tremendous resource to my office on everything from air traffic

4

control towers to the TSA and scanners. She has a proven record of success that the airport operations at Glacier have steadily increased over the past several years.

Located 6 miles northeast of Kalispell, Montana, Glacier Park International Airport is an important part of the aviation industry that supports 19,000 jobs and creates more than $1.5 billion of economic growth in Montana.

Cindi has a bachelor's degree of science in professional aeronautics in airport management from Embry-Riddle Aeronautical University. Before becoming the airport director in one of the most beautiful areas of the world—and I kid you not. If you have not been to the Flathead and been up there where Cindi manages her operation, it is indeed one of the most beautiful places in America.

Prior to being the airport director in Montana, she managed airports in Wyoming, Florida, California, and Washington, DC, metro areas. Let's just say she has seen a lot of different operations.

We are really grateful to have you in Montana and here at this hearing this morning, Cindi.

Thank you.

Mr. HUDSON. Thank you, Mr. Daines.

To continue introducing our distinguished panel today, Mr. Mark VanLoh is the director of aviation for the Kansas City Aviation Department. As director, Mr. VanLoh oversees all aspects of the management, development, operation, and maintenance of Kansas City International Airport.

Prior to his tenure in Kansas City, Mr. VanLoh served in leadership positions at other airports, including president and CEO of the Chattanooga Metropolitan Airport Authority and commissioner of airports for Cleveland Hopkins International Airport and Burke Lakefront Airport in Cleveland, Ohio.

Mr. Steve Amitay is executive director and general counsel for the National Association of Security Companies, NASCO, the Nation's largest contract security association. Mr. Amitay is also the president of Amitay Consulting, a government affairs firm in Washington, DC.

Since 2006, Mr. Amitay has led NASCO's efforts in working with Congress, Federal agencies, and the GAO on programs, legislation, and issues related to private security, in general, and, specifically, the use of private security by the Federal Government.

Mr. J. David Cox is the national president of the American Federation of Government Employees, a position he was elected to in 2012. AFGE is the largest Federal employee union, representing 650,000 Federal and D.C. Government workers Nation-wide and overseas.

AFGE provides its members with legal representation, legislative advocacy, technical expertise, and informational services. He also has ties to my home State in North Carolina.

So I appreciate all of you being here.

The witnesses' full written statements will appear in the record.

Other Members are reminded that statements may be submitted for the record.

[The statements of Ranking Member Richmond and Ranking Member Thompson follow:]

STATEMENT OF RANKING MEMBER CEDRIC L. RICHMOND

JULY 29, 2014

Thank you, Mr. Chairman.

Thank you for convening this hearing.

Today, we will have an opportunity to hear from both private-sector and Government witnesses about the Transportation Security Administration's Screening Partnership Program.

Regardless of our personal convictions about whether passenger and baggage screening should be conducted by Federal or contract screeners, we all have an interest in ensuring that TSA is operating the program efficiently and in accordance with the law.

According to TSA, the agency has approved all applications from airports opting to participate in the Screening Partnership Program since changes to the controlling law were enacted in 2012.

While I understand and appreciate concerns about how long it has taken TSA to solicit and award contracts for screening services following the initial approval of applications, my concern about this program is primarily focused on how the existing workforce is impacted.

Transportation Security Officers serve on the front lines of our fight to protect our aviation sector.

Through no fault of their own, they are subject to being left without a job or being forced to take a pay cut and lose benefits when an airport decides to opt out of using Federal screeners. TSA's decision to ignore the Department of Labor's determination that prevailing wage requirements should apply to all SPP contracts only compounds this problem.

I would humbly submit that TSA should stick to security policy and allow the Department of Labor to interpret the applicability of labor laws to Federal contracts.

By defying the Department of Labor on this issue, TSA is encouraging a race to the bottom as it relates to wages for screeners across the country.

This applies to both Federal screeners who work at airports that may opt to participate in the SPP and those with contract screeners already in place.

As contracts for screening services expire and new contracts are bid on, companies with existing contracts will be at a distinct disadvantage in submitting a competitive bid as it relates to cost.

I am hopeful that someone in the administration will step in, do the right thing, and require TSA to include prevailing wage requirements in SPP contracts.

Failing to do so will result in a return to the pre-9/11 system where screeners were compensated at the bare minimum rate, fostering rapid workforce turnover and an abundance of inexperienced screeners on the front lines.

Protecting our aviation system should be a career option, not a part-time, low-paying job.

I look forward to hearing from each of the witnesses before the subcommittee today about their views on TSA's management of the Screening Partnership Program.

Specifically, I am eager to hear the perspective of the front-line workforce from AFGE national president Cox.

As the exclusive representative for Transportation Security Officers, AFGE is uniquely positioned to understand the strains placed on the workforce when an airport opts to transition to contract screeners.

I am also looking forward to hearing from Ms. Grover about how TSA has implemented the Government Accountability Office's recommendations for improvements to the program.

Before yielding back, Mr. Chairman, I ask unanimous consent that testimony provided to the committee by John L. Martin, airport director of San Francisco International Airport, calling for TSA to comply with the Service Contract Act (SCA) and honor the current collectively-bargained rates of wages and benefits for its employees, be entered into the record.

Additionally, I ask unanimous consent to enter into the record testimony provided to the committee from Valarie Long, executive vice president of the Service Employees International Union, which expresses serious concern about the failure of TSA to comply with the Department of Labor decision regarding the Service Contract Act and points to the fundamental problems to public security that arise when employees—whether Federal or contracted—are not adequately trained and compensated.

Thank you, Mr. Chairman. I yield back the balance of my time.

STATEMENT OF RANKING MEMBER BENNIE G. THOMPSON

JULY 29, 2014

Thank you, Mr. Chairman.

And thank you for holding this hearing today.

I would also like to thank the witnesses for appearing before the subcommittee to discuss the Transportation Security Administration's Screening Partnership Program. The program at issue today, which affords airports the opportunity to return to the pre-9/11 model of using contract employees to screen passengers and baggage at our Nation's airports, tends to evoke strong passion on both sides of the aisle.

After 9/11 it was clear to the vast majority of Members of Congress and the Bush administration that transitioning to a Federal screener workforce was the right thing to do for the security of our Nation.

And, it worked. There has not been a successful attack against our aviation system on U.S. soil since 9/11. Despite that fact, Republican calls for returning to a contract screener workforce have increased in recent years.

Indeed, in 2012, the platform adopted during the Republican National Convention called for the private sector to take over airport screening wherever feasible. Some on the other side of the aisle claim that transitioning to a contract workforce results in more efficient and friendlier screeners.

This claim simply does not stand up to scrutiny. What actually happens when an airport chooses to use contract screeners is that the very same Transportation Security Officers working at the airport are recruited by the private screening company that is awarded the contract.

One day they are Federal employees with the associated benefits and employment protections and the next they are employees of a corporation, likely headquartered in a far-away State, without the security of a Federal pension in later years. How that could make the screeners more effective, efficient, or friendly is beyond comprehension.

I look forward to hearing what national president Cox has to say about Transportation Security Officers that have recently been recruited by the company that has been awarded the contract to conduct screening services at four airports in Montana. I also look forward to hearing from Mr. Cox about the strain placed on screeners when they are informed that the airport they work at will be transitioning to a contract screener workforce.

In 2012, the Government Accountability Office issued a report highlighting deficiencies in TSA's management of the Screening Partnership Program. I look forward to hearing from Ms. Grover on the steps TSA has taken to improve the management of the program and implement GAO's recommendations. Specifically, I will be interested in understanding whether TSA is providing airports that inquire about the program the information they need to make an informed decision about whether and how to apply to the program.

As for Mr. Benner, I am deeply concerned with TSA's recent decision to rebuke the Department of Labor and insist that the agency will not include prevailing wage requirements in SPP contracts. The Department of Labor directed TSA to include prevailing wage requirements in SPP contracts in June of 2013. I will be interested in hearing from Mr. Benner about why it took TSA over a year to respond to the Department of Labor and why the agency continues to ignore the directive.

Finally, I would like to point out that many of the changes made to the law controlling for entry into the Screening Partnership Program in the FAA Modernization and Reform Act of 2012 were ill-informed and should be repealed. Chief among those is the provision allowing for subsidiaries of foreign-owned corporations to compete for and be awarded contracts for screening services.

Earlier this Congress, I, along with Ranking Members Richmond and Lowey introduced the Contract Screener Reform and Accountability Act which would reinstate the law stipulating that a company could only get a contract for screening services if it was owned and controlled by a U.S. citizen.

With that Mr. Chairman, I yield back the balance of my time.

Mr. HUDSON. The Chairman now recognizes Ms. Martin to testify.

STATEMENT OF CINDI MARTIN, C.M., AIRPORT DIRECTOR, GLACIER PARK INTERNATIONAL AIRPORT

Ms. MARTIN. Chairman Hudson, Mr. Daines, thank you very much for the opportunity to share with the committee the Flathead

Municipal Airport Authority's experience with the TSA Screening Partnership application and transition process.

The Authority owns and operates Glacier Park International Airport, a Category 3 non-hub/GA airport located in northwest Montana, 20 minutes from Glacier National Park. The airport is one of 13 commercial service airports in Montana.

Currently there are five airports in eastern Montana with essential air service that participate in the Screening Partnership Program. To date, five additional Montana commercial service airports have applied to the Screening Partnership Program.

It is not a coincidence that most of the commercial service airports in Montana have applied to the program. In September and October 2007, TSA senior management came to Montana and made personal visits to every commercial service airport in the State to promote the Screening Partnership Program.

TSA management encouraged each airport to apply to the program, citing the agency's desire to be relieved of the transportation security officer human resources burden so that the agency could concentrate on regulatory compliance and oversight.

TSA's strong encouragement to apply to the program dovetailed with the Airport Authority's serious concerns about TSA's staffing levels and customer service at Glacier Park International Airport.

Prior to the decision to apply to the program, the airport's TSA staffing members had been reduced every year, despite increasing passenger traffic. In the winter of 2007, airport management was informed that the then-current staffing level was again being reduced, this time by nearly half, from 30 to 17.

Additionally, airport management consistently received complaints from the flying public about poor customer service from TSOs and long wait times, and our incumbent air carriers regularly complained about flight delays caused by slow TSA baggage and passenger screening.

In the summer of 2007, the Airport Authority invested in an expansion of the airport security checkpoint with the expectation that some of the passenger screening efficiencies would be realized, but these benefits did not materialize. Numerous appeals by the Airport Authority to TSA headquarters about staffing and customer service issues went unanswered.

Finally, in March 2008, after engaging Montana's Congressional representatives, TSA headquarters informed the airport that screener staffing at the airport was based on specific data fed into the agency's staffing allocation model based on October official airline guide data.

Although the airport receives year-round air service, we experience a large seasonal spike in passenger traffic from June through September. Passenger traffic from October through May is significantly reduced. So using October OAG flight schedules to plan for staffing at this airport is not appropriate for determining staffing levels that include the peak summer season.

Given these frustrating communications with TSA headquarters, continued staffing problems and customer service complaint issues, the Airport Authority began exploring the SPP option in earnest.

Following considerable due diligence, the Airport Authority became convinced that a private screening contractor could better serve the flying public and our air carrier partners' needs far better than TSA workforce could or would.

In October 2009, the Authority submitted its application to participate in the Screening Partnership Program in accordance with the standards in effect at the time, and then we waited.

On October 28, 2011, TSA leadership announced that TSA would not expand the Screening Partnership Program because it did not see a clear or substantial advantage to expanding the program and that the pending applications from five airports were denied.

Thus, without visiting, consulting, or communicating with the Airport Authority or providing any substantive justification for its decision, TSA summarily sent the Airport Authority a letter denying our application.

Numerous appeals by the Airport Authority to TSA headquarters and leadership inquiring about the new standard and the metrics used to justify the denial of our application went unanswered.

In the spring of 2012, TSA announced that there was a new application and process for applying to the program. I personally was contacted by the SPP office and encouraged to submit a new application.

The instructions to TSA's new application form state that, "Given the level of participation in the current program, and in order to maximize TSA's effectiveness as a Federal counterterrorism security agency, TSA is not inclined at this time to expand the Screening Partnership Program unless there are clear and substantial advantages to do so."

The instructions go on to state that, "Therefore, your application must explain how private screening at your airport will provide those clear and substantial advantages, while maintaining our high standards and meeting the threats of today and the future."

Despite the fact that the airport never received an answer as to the substantive—the specific substantive reasons the first application was denied or even the substantive criteria against which the new application would be measured, we applied again on April 6, 2012.

At approximately the same time, three other airport—Montana airports—reapplied to the Screening Partnership Program: Bozeman, Butte, and West Yellowstone. Missoula International Airport, whose application had been denied in January 2011, did not reapply.

In October 2012, the four Montana airports were informed that a request for proposal for SPP services at our airports was being issued. The RFP was released on October 23, 2012, with responses due on November 26, 2012.

In mid-January 2013, the Montana airports were informed that the contract was being—award was being pushed back to late February 2013. Initial indication of a contract award was made by TSA to the four Montana airports in March 2013 and then, without warning or explanation or—the solicitation was canceled on April 17, 2013. There was no official reason offered by TSA for the cancellation, nor were we given any time line for the reissuance of an RFP.

On August 30, 2013, the four Montana airports were notified that a second RFP for SPP services were being issued and that re-

9

sponses were due by September 30, 2013. On November 13, 2013, we were informed via email that the response date had been pushed back to November 19, 2013.

Finally, on May 30, 2014, the four Montana airports that had applied to SPP program were notified that an SPP contract had been awarded effective June 1, 2014, and that the transition to SPP contractor would occur within 90 days, that is, by August 29, 2014, 4 years and 10 months after our first application to the program.

Within days of the official notification of the award, the SPP contractor was on site at our airport. While the transition period has not been without a few hiccups, we are seeing light at the end of what has been a very long tunnel.

The Authority's decision to apply for SPP was not made lightly. It was made in the best interest of the flying public, our air carrier partners, and the community. Despite the frustrating length of time through the fits and starts of this process and the lack of communication from TSA, we would do it all again.

We believe in the Screening Partnership Program and firmly believe that SPP is the right choice for Glacier Park International Airport.

That concludes my prepared statement, Mr. Chairman. I would be happy to answer any questions.

[The prepared statement of Ms. Martin follows:]

PREPARED STATEMENT OF CINDI MARTIN

Chairman Hudson, Ranking Member Richmond, and Members of the subcommittee: Thank you for the opportunity to share with the committee the Flathead Municipal Airport Authority's experience with the TSA Screening Partnership Program (SPP) application and transition process. The Authority owns and operates Glacier Park International Airport, a Category 3, non-hub/GA airport located in Northwest Montana—20 minutes from Glacier National Park.

The airport is one of 13 commercial service airports in Montana. Currently there are 5 airports in eastern Montana with essential air service (EAS) that participate in the Screening Partnership Program (SPP) and to-date 5 additional Montana commercial service airports have applied to the Screening Partnership Program (SPP).

It is not a coincidence that most of the commercial service airports in Montana have applied to the program.

In September and October of 2007, TSA senior management came to Montana and made personal visits to every commercial service airport in the State to promote the Screening Partnership Program. TSA management encouraged each airport to apply to the Program, citing the agency's desire to be relieved of the Transportation Security Officer (TSO) human resources burden so that the agency could concentrate on regulatory compliance and oversight.

TSA's strong encouragement to apply to the program dovetailed with the Airport Authority's serious concerns about TSA staffing levels and customer service at Glacier Park International Airport.

Prior to the decision to apply to the program, the airport's TSA staffing numbers had been reduced every year, despite increasing passenger traffic. And, in the winter of 2007, airport management was informed that the then-current staffing level was again being reduced, this time by nearly half—from 30 to 17. Additionally, airport management consistently received complaints from the flying public about poor customer service from TSOs and long wait times, and incumbent air carriers regularly complained about flight delays caused by slow TSA baggage and passenger screening.

In the summer of 2007, the Airport Authority invested in an expansion of the airport's security checkpoint with the expectation that some passenger screening efficiencies would be realized, but these benefits did not materialize.

Numerous appeals by the Airport Authority to TSA headquarters about staffing and customer service issues went unanswered. Finally in March 2008, after engaging Montana's Congressional representatives, TSA headquarters informed the airport that screener staffing at the airport was based upon specific data fed into the agency's Staffing Allocation Model (SAM) based on October Official Airline Guide (OAG) data.

Although the airport receives year-round air carrier service, we experience a large seasonal spike in passenger traffic from June through September. Passenger traffic from October through May is significantly reduced, and so using October OAG flight schedules to plan for staffing at this airport is not appropriate for determining staffing levels that include the peak summer season.

Given these frustrating communications with TSA headquarters, continued staffing problems, and customer complaint issues, the Airport Authority began exploring the SPP option in earnest. Following considerable due diligence, the Airport Authority became convinced that a private screening contractor could better serve the flying public and our air carrier partners' needs far better than the TSA workforce could or would.

THE AUTHORITY'S SPP APPLICATION

In October 2009, the Authority submitted its application to participate in the Screening Partnership Program in accordance with the standards in effect at the time.

And then we waited.

On January 28, 2011, TSA leadership announced that TSA would not expand the Screening Partnership Program, because it did not see a clear or substantial advantage to expanding the program, and that the pending applications from 5 airports were denied. Thus, without visiting, consulting, or communicating with the Airport Authority, or providing any substantive justification for its decision, TSA summarily sent the Airport Authority a letter denying our application.

Numerous appeals by the Airport Authority to TSA headquarters and leadership inquiring about the new standard and the metrics used to justify the denial of our application went unanswered.

In the spring of 2012, TSA announced that there was a new application and process for applying to the program. I was contacted by the SPP office and encouraged to submit a new application.

The instructions to TSA's new application form state that "Given the level of participation in the current program, and in order to maximize TSA's effectiveness as a Federal counterterrorism security agency, TSA is not inclined at this time to expand the Screening Partnership Program unless there are clear and substantial advantages to do so." The instructions go on to state that "Therefore, your application must explain how private screening at your airport will provide those clear and substantial advantages, while maintaining our high standards and meeting the threats of today and the future."

Despite the fact that the airport never received an answer as to the specific substantive reasons its first application was denied—or even the substantive criteria against which the new application would be measured—we applied again, on April 6, 2012. At approximately the same time, three other Montana airports re-applied to the Screening Partnership Program—Bozeman, Butte, and West Yellowstone. The Missoula International Airport, whose application had been denied in January 2011, did not reapply.

In October 2012, the four Montana airports were informed that a Request for Proposal (RFP) for SPP services at our airports was being issued. The RFP was released on October 23, 2012, with responses due on November 26, 2012.

In mid-January 2013 the Montana airports were informed that the contract award was being pushed back to late February 2013.

Initial indication of a contract award was made by TSA to the four Montana airports in March 2013. And, then without warning or explanation, the solicitation was canceled on April 17, 2013.

There was no official reason offered by TSA for the cancelation, nor were we given a time line for the reissuance of an RFP.

On August 30, 2013 the four Montana airports were notified that a second RFP for SPP services had been issued and that responses were due by September 30, 2013.

On November 13, 2013 we were informed, via email, that the response due date had been pushed back to November 19, 2013.

And, finally, on May 30, 2014, the four Montana airports that had applied to the SPP program were notified that an SPP contract had been awarded effective June 1, 2014, and, that the transition to the SPP contractor would occur within 90 days— that is, by August 29, 2014.

Four years and 10 months after our first application to the program.

Within days of the official notification of the award, the SPP contractor was onsite at our airport. And while the transition period has not been without a few hiccups, we are seeing light at the end of what has been a very long tunnel.

The Authority's decision to apply for SPP was not made lightly—it was made in the best interest of the flying public, our air carrier partners and the community. And, despite the frustrating length of time through the fits and starts of the process and the lack of communication from TSA, we would do it all again. We believe in the Screening Partnership Program, and firmly believe that SPP is right for Glacier Park International Airport.

That concludes my prepared statement, Mr. Chairman. I would be happy to answer any questions you or the other subcommittee Members may have.

Mr. HUDSON. Thank you, Ms. Martin.

The Chairman recognizes Mr. VanLoh to testify.

STATEMENT OF MARK VANLOH, A.A.E., AVIATION DEPARTMENT, KANSAS CITY INTERNATIONAL AIRPORT

Mr. VANLOH. Good morning, Mr. Chairman, and Members of the Transportation Security Committee.

My name is Mark VanLoh. I am the director of aviation for the city of Kansas City, Missouri. Thank you for inviting me to appear today before you.

First I would like to describe Kansas City International Airport. It is one of the country's major medium hubs and serves approximately 10 million annual passengers. Though it was designed in the late 1960s, it has three separate semi-circular passenger terminals that are not connected.

The lack of a central concourse also creates the need for multiple security screening locations and does not allow a central screening checkpoint that is common with most modern airports. Several hundred screeners at several checkpoints are employed to perform passenger screening in Kansas City.

My testimony today addresses the Screening Partnership Program based upon Kansas City's nearly 12 years of experience in this program. Kansas City was selected by TSA in 2002 under the pilot program, along with San Francisco, Rochester, Tupelo, and Jackson Hole. It is a partnership that has worked extremely well in Kansas City.

I have been an airport operator for 30 years and, in my view, the Screening Partnership Program has provided a level of screening services and security protection at least as good as and, we think, better than that TSA would have provided using Federal personnel, and it has done so with operational efficiency and high levels of customer satisfaction.

My counterparts at other airports are often envious of our service record and security, and I am always happy to brag about it.

Often I am asked by the flying public what exactly does an airport director do and what does my typical day consist of. It is not spent on security, it is not spent on safety, and it is not spent negotiating with airlines.

It is dealing with 500 employees and their personnel issues, performance reviews, labor relations, grievance hearings, disciplinary actions, family medical leave, random drug screening reviews, and other personnel issues. I can't imagine, with over 50,000 employees, what kind of time TSA spends on these issues.

In my opinion, the majority of these efforts by TSA should be focused on intelligence gathering to reduce the threat against aviation and then issuing policy and procedures to protect our industry, not on personnel issues.

At Kansas City, the SPP provider handles all of the personnel issues, leaving TSA to oversee security. The operator and overseer are different entities. This results in built-in accountability and allows each to do what they can and should do best.

The advantage of the SPP program can be summarized as follows. Enhanced flexibility and efficiencies in personnel use and deployment. Greater flexibility to respond to increased or decreased service requirements at the checkpoints. Greater flexibility to cross-train and cross-utilize employees not subject to the Federal employee hiring freeze and employment caps.

As an aside, during the recent sequestration, while other airports with Federal staff were subject to Federal regulations, we in Kansas City operated normally with no disruptions.

More effective in dealing with non-performers. This may sound a bit harsh and insensitive, but we all know that the job requires an inordinate amount of attention and personnel skills. Occasionally, an employee may be hired that shouldn't be in that position.

We can all tell the screeners at airports that enjoy their job and they are good at it. The SPP provider is able to make changes with minimal disruption to the mission. A high degree of customer service awareness is critical. We all want our passengers to enjoy their time in our airports.

The private screening company has greater flexibility than the Federal Government to redeploy screeners on short notice, to reschedule screener shifts to and from off-hours, and to add or delete security checkpoints on short notice.

It has been great from the beginning in Kansas City, but lately it has caused me great concern, given the issues with the rebidding of our contract.

We are now almost 4 years outside the expiration of the recent contract in Kansas City. Even though the uncertainty of not knowing if they will have a job after each holiday season, our screeners have maintained a high level of service and dedication.

It is my understanding that this solicitation is now in a Court of Federal Claims court for the third time. The low bidder selected by TSA included across-the-board pay cuts, as well as cuts in hours, to all of our screeners now working in Kansas City.

Meanwhile, TSA recently announced pay raises for Federal screeners at other airports, but then selected this low bidder in Kansas City based on this treatment of our existing workforce.

Even with the contract award issues, I firmly believe the program has worked well in Kansas City. There are a number of areas in which I think the program could be improved. Mr. Chairman, you mentioned a few of them.

TSA needs to be more flexible in its supervision of private screening companies as to better foster improvements in innovation. TSA should set minimum levels of security standards, but give the private screeners the flexibility to provide the screening in new and different and innovative and creative ways.

However, as we understand it, TSA requires Federal and private screeners to operate under the same procedures, including centralization procedures for hiring and assessments and coordination through their headquarters. I do not believe the law requires a one-size-fits-all approach.

Second, the TSA should develop staffing resources based on the operational requirements of each airport and not arbitrarily system-wide based on staffing caps. Such an approach would be more effective to account for the unique requirements of each airport, including part-time and efficient full-time screeners.

Again, one size doesn't fit all. For example, staffing requirements at Kansas City International, which does not have a single security checkpoint location, will be markedly different than other requirements for other airports.

Third, there needs to be greater coordination with the airport operator. More can be done to get the operator's input in the operational procedures, staffing, and other critical activities.

For example, in TSA's contested contract award that I mentioned above, TSA recently chose to replace Kansas City's long-time private screening company through the bid process, yet, never asked us our input on the incumbent's prior performance.

Fourth, the choice of screening company should be based largely on technical capabilities and performance, not on cost. Basing selection primarily on cost considerations will return us to the poorly performing system pre-9/11 where contract screeners who—lacked experience, critical skills, and performance incentives. TSA needs to ensure that the selection is truly a best value.

In conclusion, the Screening Partnership Program has worked well in Kansas City. It has shown that private screeners under the direct oversight of the TSA will perform excellent security and customer service at reasonable costs.

Mr. Chairman, this concludes my prepared remarks. I would be happy to address any questions you and the Members may have. Thank you.

[The prepared statement of Mr. VanLoh follows:]

PREPARED STATEMENT OF MARK VANLOH

JULY 29, 2014

Good afternoon, Mr. Chairman and Members of the Transportation Security Subcommittee. My name is Mark VanLoh and I am the director of aviation for the city of Kansas City, Missouri. Thank you for inviting me to appear before you today to discuss the Airport Screener Partnership Program.

First, I want to describe Kansas City International Airport. It is one the country's major medium-hub airports and serves approximately 10 million annual passengers. Designed in the late 1960's, it has three separate semi-circular passenger terminals that are not connected. The lack of a central concourse also creates the need for multiple security screening locations and does not allow for central security screening that is common with more modern airports. Several hundred screeners at several checkpoints are employed to perform passenger screening.

My testimony today addresses the Screener Partnership Program based upon Kansas City's nearly 12 years of experience under the program since it began in 2002.

Kansas City was selected by TSA in 2002 under the "pilot program" along with 4 other airports—San Francisco, Rochester, Tupelo, and Jackson Hole.

It is a partnership that has worked extremely well at Kansas City. I have been an airport operator for 30 years, and in my view the Screening Partnership Program has provided a level of screening services and security protection at least as good as, we think better than, the levels that TSA would have provided using Federal personnel. And, it has done so with operational efficiency and high levels of customer satisfaction. My counterparts at other airports are often envious of our record of service and security. I am always pleased to brag about it.

Often I am asked by the public what an airport director does and on what issue we spend the most time during a normal day. It is not security or safety or airline negotiations but employee issues. With 500 employees, a considerable portion of the day consists of employee performance reviews, labor relations/grievance hearings, disciplinary actions, family medical leaves, random drug screening reviews, and other personnel issues. I cannot imagine what amount of time is consumed by TSA with over 50,000 employees. In my opinion, the majority of efforts by the TSA should be focused on intelligence gathering to reduce the threat against aviation and then issuing policy and procedures to protect our industry not on personnel issues. At Kansas City, the SPP provider handles all the personnel issues leaving TSA to oversee security. The operator and overseer are different entities. This results in built-in accountability and allows each do what they can and should do best.

The advantages of the Screening Partnership Program can be summarized as follows:

- enhanced flexibility and efficiencies in personnel use and deployment.
- greater flexibility to respond to increased or decreased service requirements.
- greater flexibility to cross-train and cross-utilize personnel.
- not subject to Federal employee "hiring freezes" and employment caps. As an aside, during the recent sequestration, while other airports with Federal staff were subjected to Federal restrictions, we at Kansas City operated normally with no disruptions.
- More effective in dealing with non-performers. This may sound a bit insensitive but we all know that the job requires an inordinate amount of attention and personal skills. Occasionally an employee may be hired that probably shouldn't be in that position. We can all tell the screeners that enjoy their job and want to be there. The SPP provider is able to make changes with minimal disruption to the mission. A high degree of customer service awareness is critical. We all want our passengers to enjoy their airport experience.

The private screening company has greater flexibility than the Federal Government to re-deploy screeners on short notice, to reschedule screener shifts to and from off-hours, and to add or delete screening checkpoints on short notice.

Based on our nearly 12 years of experience under the private screening program, I can report that the Screening Partnership Program has been very effective in providing high-quality service to our passengers at a level of security equal to, if not better than, the level that would be provided at the airport using Federal Government employees.

The SPP has been great for Kansas City from the beginning, but has caused me great concern lately given the issues surrounding the rebid of the contract. We are now almost 4 years outside the expiration of the most recent contract. Even through the uncertainty of not knowing if they will have a job after each holiday season, our screeners have maintained their high level of service and dedication. It is my understanding that this solicitation is now in the Court of Federal Claims for the third time. The low bidder selected by TSA included across-the-board pay cuts as well as cuts in hours to all screeners now working at the airport. Meanwhile TSA recently announced pay raises for Federal screeners at other airports but selected this low bidder in Kansas City based on this treatment of our existing workforce.

Even with the contract award issues, I firmly believe the program has worked well for Kansas City; there are a number of areas in which the program could be improved.

First, TSA needs to be more flexible in its supervision of private-screening companies so as to better foster improvements and innovation. TSA should set minimum levels of security standards and operational procedures, but give the private screeners the flexibility to provide the security in new, different, innovative, and creative ways. However, as we understand it, TSA requires Federal and private screeners to operate under the same procedures, including centralized procedures for screener hiring and assessments, and coordination or hiring through TSA headquarters. I do not believe that the law requires a one-size-fits-all approach.

Second, TSA should develop staffing resources based on the operational requirements for each airport, not on arbitrary system-wide staffing caps based on the National models it uses for the Federal workforce. Such an approach would more effectively account for the unique requirements of each airport, including part-time and efficient full-time screener schedules. Again, one size doesn't fit all. For example, staffing requirements for Kansas City International Airport, which does not have a single central security location, will be markedly different than the requirements for airports that have centralized security screening facilities.

Third, there needs to be greater coordination with the airport operator. More can be done to get the airport operator's input in the operational procedures, staffing, and other critical activities. For example in TSA's contested contract award that I mentioned above, TSA recently chose to replace Kansas City's long-time private screening company through the bid process, yet never asked Kansas City for our input on the incumbent's prior performance.

Fourth, the choice of screening companies should be based largely on technical capabilities and performance, not on cost. Basing selection primarily on cost considerations we will return us to the poorly performing system that existed pre-9/11 where contracts were generally awarded to the lowest-cost bidder, manned by screeners who lacked experience, critical skills, and performance incentives. TSA needs to ensure that the selection is truly a "best value".

In conclusion, the Screening Partnership Program has worked well at Kansas City International Airport. It has shown that private screeners under the direct oversight of the TSA will perform excellent security and customer service and at reasonable costs. Mr. Chairman, this concludes my prepared remarks. I would be pleased to address any questions you and the Members of the subcommittee may have.

Mr. HUDSON. Thank you, Mr. VanLoh.

The Chairman will now recognize Mr. Amitay to testify.

STATEMENT OF STEVE AMITAY, ESQ., EXECUTIVE DIRECTOR/GENERAL COUNSEL, NATIONAL ASSOCIATION OF SECURITY COMPANIES

Mr. AMITAY. Thank you, Mr. Chairman.

Chairman Hudson, Congressman Daines, my name is Steve Amitay, and I am executive director and general counsel to NASCO, National Association of Security Companies.

Founded in 1972, NASCO is the Nation's largest contract security trade association whose member companies employ more than 300,000 armed and unarmed security officers across the Nation.

More specifically, NASCO members are providing security and screening services throughout the Federal Government for DHS agencies, the CIA, the FBI, NASA, the Federal judiciary, National labs and nuclear sites, and military installations, and at U.S. airports through the TSA Screening Partnership Program.

The subject of today's hearing is to examine TSA's management of the now 12-year-old Screening Partnership Program, if you count the 2 pilot years, which was created in the Aviation Transportation Security Act, or ATSA, which also stood up TSA.

However, despite its successful operation these past 12 years, as Mark has just noted, some still like to make the uninformed base assertion that private screeners should not be used at airports.

Well, putting aside that the use of private screeners allows TSA to focus more on aviation security and less on personnel management and putting aside that OMB does not consider such screening services to be inherently Governmental and putting aside that all cargo screening in the United States is done by private companies under TSA oversight and putting aside that virtually all other Western countries have determined that private screening under Government oversight is the most effective screening model, by law, SPP private screeners must meet the same employment, proficiency, and training requirements of Federal screeners and all the security screening conducted by private screening companies must be done in accordance with all TSA standard operating procedures and operational directives related to screening functions.

No one has ever found that private screeners are not as effective as Federal screeners. On the contrary, the limited available evidence shows the opposite. As for cost, as with many other services, the evidence is overwhelming that the private sector is less costly.

While there are serious questions about TSA's interpretation of the compensation requirement of ATSA, which can lower private screener costs, I would like to note that there are also some seriously false statements being made about the compensation being offered as part of the current conversion of several Montana airports from Federal screening to the SPP.

First, the wages for those Federal screeners who remain will not be changed. Second, the health plan being offered by the contractor does indeed allow for screeners to use in-network providers in Montana through the Blue Cross Blue Shield system of State associations, thus making the plan competitive and available.

Getting back to performance and cost comparisons, in the fiscal year 2014 Consolidated Appropriations Act, TSA is directed to fund an independent performance comparison that shall include security effectiveness, cost, throughput, wait times, management efficiencies, customer satisfaction, and other elements.

NASCO relishes such an independent study and, if accurate and comprehensive comparisons of the costs of all screeners to the Federal Government between Federal and private is conducted, NASCO believes private screeners would fare very, very well.

NASCO would also like to see comparisons of attrition, absenteeism, and injury rates, which are huge cost-drivers and affect performance. The GAO has sought this, too. As GAO noted in its 2013 report on TSA screener misconduct, of the 9,600 cases of misconduct from 2010 through 2012, the No. 1 category accounting for 32 percent of the cases was attendance and leave-related misconduct.

Private screening companies employ robust attendance policies and other screener oversights that reduces absenteeism, thereby decreasing cost and increasing performance.

The program, though, does face serious obstacles as a result of two incredibly questionable interpretations of governing law by TSA.

First, TSA believes the Federal screening cost estimate, or FCE, which sets the required cost-efficiency price ceiling for private screening bids, only has to contain Federal screener cost borne by TSA and not all the Federal or taxpayer cost.

Second, as to the requirement that private screener compensation be "no less than such Government personnel," here TSA believes that private screening companies do not have to pay compensation to their screeners that is equivalent with such Federal screeners, but only that they must pay screeners the minimum or starting Federal screener wages.

How TSA believes that its contracts for screening services are not subject to the Service Contract Act, even though all other Federal agencies' screening and security services contracts are subject to the SCA, is confounding. Both these interpretations fly in the face of a plain reading of the statute, the intent of Congress, and public security policy. They are both major threats to the program that detrimentally affect the acquisition and award process.

The first interpretation concerning the FCE creates artificially low-bid ceilings, and the second concerning the minimum pay requirements encourages unnecessary low bids. Such a policy is not good for airports, screeners, companies, and passengers, and, most of all, it is not at all justified under the law.

As detailed in my written testimony, if TSA's FCEs are accurate and the compensation requirement is enforced as meaning equivalent compensation, there are still many cost savings related to screener management and oversight and scheduling administration and basic differences between the private and public sector services world that enable private companies to operate at a lower cost, including with a small profit, but with at least the same required performance as Federal screeners.

If TSA will not address the problems associated with these issues, then Congress should step in as it did when TSA used another questionable interpretation of the statutory language related to the application approval process to improve—to impede the program in the past.

Thank you.

[The prepared statement of Mr. Amitay follows:]

PREPARED STATEMENT OF STEVE AMITAY

JULY 29, 2014

NASCO AND PRIVATE SECURITY

NASCO is the Nation's largest contract security trade association, whose member companies employ more than 300,000 security officers. Across the Nation almost 2 million private security officers, both contract and proprietary are at work protecting (and often screening persons and bags) at Federal buildings, courthouses, military installations, critical infrastructure facilities, businesses, schools, and public areas. In addition, as the Screening Partnership Program (SPP) has demonstrated, private companies are also effectively providing passenger and baggage screening services to U.S. airports. Formed in 1972, NASCO strives to increase awareness and understanding among policy-makers, consumers, the media, and the general public of the important role of private security in safeguarding persons and property. At the same time, NASCO has been the leading advocate for raising standards for the licensing of private security firms and the registration, screening, and training of security officers. At every level of government, NASCO has worked with legislators and officials to put in place higher standards for companies and officers.

Over the past decade, NASCO has provided input to and worked with Congress, GAO, Federal agencies and others on issues and programs related to the use of contract security by Federal agencies. NASCO has been involved with the SPP virtually since its inception and NASCO has also been very active in working with Congress and the Federal Protective Service (FPS) to strengthen the "public-private partnership" that is the FPS Protective Security Officer Program which utilizes approximately 13,500 contract security officers to protect Federal building within the GSA portfolio.

BACKGROUND ON THE SPP

After 9/11 Congress passed the Aviation and Transportation Security Act (ATSA), which stood up TSA and authorized it to assume responsibility for security in all modes of transportation, including the creation of a Federal workforce to conduct passenger and baggage screening at U.S. airports. However, Congress did not make a blanket judgment that in going forward with more stringent airport screening only a Federal workforce could provide effective screening. ATSA also required TSA to conduct a pilot program with up to five airports, one from each of the five "airport security risk categories," where the screening would be conducted by personnel from a qualified private screening company chosen by TSA operating under strict Federal standards, supervision, and oversight. At the conclusion of the successful pilot in 2004, TSA created the "Screening Partnership Program" which allows any airport to apply to "opt out" of using Federal screeners and instead use a qualified private screening selected and overseen by TSA.

Currently, there are 18 airports, including all five of the airports in the original pilot program, in the SPP. By far the largest in the program is San Francisco International Airport (SFO) in California and the second largest is Kansas City International Airport (KCI) in Missouri. It is expected that soon awards will be made for the Orlando Sanford (SFB) and Sarasota (SRQ) airports in Florida, which will be the largest airports in the program's history to transition from Federal screeners to private screeners. (While SFO and MCI are larger airports, since they were in the pilot program, they never had Federal screeners). NASCO hopes that for Orlando Sanford and Sarasota and any other airport joining the SPP, that the TSA will take the necessary steps and actions needed to provide for a smooth transition from Federal screeners to private screeners (many of whom will likely make the transition to the private sector), and avoid causing problems for the airport, the screeners, and travelers.

For a company to be "qualified to provide screening services" under the SPP, the company must only employ individuals "who meet all the requirements . . . applicable to Federal Government personnel who perform screening services at airports." The company must "provide compensation and other benefits to such individuals that are not less than the level of compensation and other benefits provided to such Federal Government personnel." Finally, a private company can only provide screening at an airport if TSA determines and certifies to Congress that "the level of screening services and protection provided at the airport under the contract will be equal to or greater than the level that would be provided at the airport by Federal Government personnel."[1]

To reiterate, at SPP airports where private screening companies are used it is required by law that: (1) The screeners at a minimum have met the same employment screening, proficiency, and training requirements of Federal screeners, (2) the screeners are provided compensation and benefits at a level no less than such Federal screeners, and (3) the level of screening services and protection provided by the company must be equal to or greater than the level that would be provided at the airport by Federal screeners.

TSA fully acknowledges that these requirements are being met. At a January Congressional hearing on the SPP in the House Oversight and Government Reform Subcommittee on Government Operations, Kelly Hoggan, Assistant Administrator, Office of Security Operations for TSA testified that "These private-sector employees [SPP screeners] were, and remain, subject to the qualification and compensation criteria of Federal Transportation Security Officers (TSOs)."[2] And on the TSA website in the material on the SPP, TSA states, "private screening airports use the same technology and follow the same procedures as Federal screening airports. Data from covert testing has confirmed that the performance for Federal and privatized screening is comparable."[3]

Therefore, when opponents of the program characterize the SPP as "a return to the pre-9/11 screening workforce of low paid and poorly trained non-Federal employees" such criticisms are blatant falsehoods and/or show a complete lack of understanding of how the SPP operates and is governed.[4]

Furthermore, while equating present-day SPP private screeners to pre-9/11 private screeners is specious comparison, the underlying accusation that private screeners are to blame for the tragedy of 9/11 is also blatantly wrong. FAA regulations in place on 9/11 permitted the weapons the terrorists used to take over the planes to be brought on board, and the 9/11 Commission Report found that each security layer relevant to hijackings—intelligence, passenger prescreening, checkpoint screening, and on-board security—was seriously flawed prior to 9/11.

In fact, over the past 12 years since airports have been using private screeners under the pre-SPP pilot and the SPP there is considerable evidence from covert testing results, GAO reports, independent evaluations, reports from airport operators, anecdotal information, and other sources that show that the public-private partnership of utilizing private screeners under Federal regulation and oversight is a superior and more cost-effective screening option for airports than using Federal screeners.[5]

---

[1] *Aviation Transportation and Security Act* Section 108 49 USC 44920.
[2] Testimony of Kelly C. Hoggan, Asst. Administrator for Security Operations House Oversight and Government Reform Hearing "TSA Oversight: Examining the Screening Partnership Program" January 14, 2014 Serial Number 113–95.
[3] TSA Website Screening Partnership Program FAQ's.
[4] *The TSO Voice;* January 20, 2010, statement of former AFGE head John Gage.
[5] See, *House Committee on Transportation and Infrastructure Oversight and Investigations, Staff Report: TSA Ignores More Cost Effective Screening Model,* June 3, 2011.

19

ISSUES AND PROBLEMS RELATED TO TSA'S MANAGEMENT OF THE SPP

In the decade the SPP has been in operation, airports, and screening companies have encountered a variety of obstacles, mis-steps, and questionable statutory interpretations on the part of TSA that have hindered the program. Some of these problems have been addressed by Congress and/or TSA but others continue to impede the growth of the program and even threaten the viability of the program.

As will be discussed in detail the two major issues impacting the SPP are:

(1) TSA's questionable interpretation of the statutory language that requires TSA to estimate the costs of Federal screening at an airport (called the Federal Cost Estimate) to set a "cost-efficiency" price ceiling for private screening at that airport. TSA believes that it only needs to consider Federal screener costs borne by TSA and its budget, and not all the Federal (taxpayer costs) of Federal screening at an airport. In addition, the accuracy of the costs that TSA uses in calculating the FCE and doing Federal/private cost comparisons are an issue.

(2) TSA's questionable interpretation of statutory language that requires private screening companies provide screeners with compensation "no less than such Government personnel." Here, TSA believes that the intent was not that screeners working for private screening companies must receive equal (or better) compensation than Federal screeners, but essentially the opposite, private screening companies only are required to pay screeners the minimum/starting TSA wages.

Both these interpretations fly in the face of a plain reading of the statute, the intent of Congress, and good public safety and fiscal policy. They are both major threats to the program. If TSA will not address the problems associated with these issues, then Congress should step in, as it did in the past, when TSA took it upon itself to impede the program through a very questionable interpretation of the statutory language related to the application approval process.

While many airports are content with their Federal screening force, and Federal screeners by and large are performing their duties satisfactorily, airport screening is not an inherently Government function, nor is it a unique security function. Many Federal agencies, including other DHS agencies, are efficiently and effectively using contract security for screening and other security services.[6] As will be fully detailed, even when private screening companies are required to provide equivalent compensation package of wages and benefits to their screeners, and even accounting for profit, they can still be more cost-efficient and more effective than Federal screeners.

SPP APPLICATION AND RFP PROCESS

As alluded to above, one of the greatest obstacles that faced that program that has now been resolved by Congress was TSA's former policy on application approvals. From around 2009 to 2012 TSA had an unstated and then stated policy to not approve new airports for the SPP unless "a clear and substantial advantage to do so emerges in the future." While the justifications for this policy were unsubstantiated and the policy seemed to contradict Congressional intent; nonetheless, it led to 5 out 6 airport SPP applications being denied and/or held up for years during that period. The policy was overruled by Congress with the enactment of the 2012 FAA Modernization Act which required TSA to approve an application within 60 days unless the approval would "compromise security or detrimentally affect the cost-efficiency or the effectiveness of the screening of passengers or property at the airport.[7] However, TSA's interpretation of this language, which added the cost-efficiency element, created the follow-on problem mentioned above and discussed later.

Currently, with the new application approval requirement in place and with TSA taking other steps to improve the application process (as recommended by Congress and GAO) the SPP application approval process is no longer problematic.

TSA and the new SPP leadership are also to be commended for their public commitment, made earlier this year, to award SPP contracts within 1 year of an application being approved. This goal is evidently in line with the wishes of Congress

---

[6] Not including the military services, there are approximately 35,000 contract security officers deployed at Federal facilities. The largest amount of contract security officers work for FPS (approx. 13,500), the United States Marshal Service (approx. 5,000), and the Department of Energy (approx. 5,000). Other Federal agencies/instrumentalities that use contact security include: IRS, NASA, FAA, USDA, DOT, DOC, HHS, SSA, NARA, DOL, FDIC, U.S. Coast Guard, State, DIA, NRC, Holocaust Museum, and Smithsonian. Federal agencies have consistently and successfully utilized private security and screening services at Level 4 and 5 secured facilities, DoD locations requiring Top Secret and above clearances, the Department of Homeland Security Headquarters, NASA launch sites, nuclear facilities, Federal Courts, military installations, and FBI offices around the country.

[7] See Pub. L. No. 112–95, §830(a), 126 Stat. 11, 135 (2012) (codified at 49 U.S.C. §44920(b)).

as in the House Report accompanying the fiscal year 2015 DHS Appropriations Bill that was passed by the House last month, the committee stated "The time taken by TSA to approve applications, issue contract solicitations, and make contract awards is unacceptable. Accordingly, TSA is directed to award applicable SPP contracts not later than 12 months from the date of receipt of such airport applications."[8] Currently, TSA is slated to make an award for Orlando Sanford Airport next month (26 months after application approval) and to make an award for Sarasota Bradenton Airport in September (17 months after application approval.) Obviously, the next SPP application approved will put the 1-year time requirement to the test.

Unfortunately, the solicitation and award process for the past several SPP RFP's have been plagued by problems involving questionable provisions, unexplainable adjustments, improper evaluations, and other issues—besides the underlying FCE and minimum pay issues—that have caused serious confusion, delays, pre-award protests, and set up the eventual awards for successful bid protests. These incidents raise concerns about TSA's ability to manage the procurement process and its commitment to the program.

TSA's handling of the SPP contract for Kansas City International (MCI) is a prime example. Kansas City was an original pilot SPP airport and in 2010 the airport's SPP contract was put out for bid. TSA made an award but it was then successfully protested and voided in the U.S. Court of Federal Claims in 2011. The Court found that TSA "failed to perform a best-value tradeoff analysis as required under the RFP; and (2) that the SSA failed to exercise and document her independent judgment in accordance with FAR 15.308." The TSA award was "essentially made on a lowest-cost technically acceptable basis not pursuant to the best-value determination required by the RFP." The procurement errors were "significant" and the Court found the award to be "arbitrary, capricious, an abuse of discretion, or otherwise not in accordance with law."[9]

In 2012 TSA issued a new RFP for Kansas City. In the new RFP, TSA included a small business participation "goal" of 40% of the total contract value. In all past SPP RFP's that included a small business participation goal the amount was a percentage of the sub-contracting total not total contract value. The Federal Acquisition Regulations (FAR) also reference small business goals in terms of a percentage of total subcontracting dollars. This unusual and excessive set-aside "goal" seemed to violate the FAR, and also contracting laws which require goals to be based on market research. More so, when TSA was asked for the RFP record "[i]s it the TSA's intent that all large businesses [be] mandated to have, as a minimum, 40% small business participation . . . as part of their overall bid?" TSA answered in the affirmative. And in other places too within the RFP the goal was characterized as mandatory.[10]

After the set-aside provision was challenged in court in a pre-bid protest, TSA quickly changed its above mentioned answer to say the goal was not mandatory. And while the Court said it "agrees with Plaintiff that the placement of this language under the heading of "Compliance/Responsiveness" is in tension with TSA's otherwise abundantly clear assertion that the 40 percent small business participation standard constitutes a goal," the Court accepted TSA's word it would change that language too.[11]

The Court then looked at the issue of the amount of the "goal" and while the Court upheld it as being legal, the Court stated, "If the Court were issuing this solicitation instead of this agency, it may well have based the rather aggressive small business goals on more robust market research, and it likely would have stated the goals as a percentage of subcontracting dollars, as FAR Part 19 authorizes."[12]

In the next open solicitation that TSA put out (Sanford) the small business goal included was a percentage of subcontracting dollars (as it had been in past RFP's), and not total contracting dollars. Again, this example shows either sloppiness or a misunderstanding of the SPP RFP process on the part of TSA and caused unnecessary delays and litigation.

The Kansas City contract was finally awarded earlier this year, but once again it has been protested in the U.S. Court of Federal Claims where it is currently being litigated.

The Kansas City contract award has not been the only troubled SPP award. In its June 2013 Report on the SPP, the DHS OIG found that "From January 2011 to August 2012, TSA did not comply fully with Federal Acquisition Regulation Sec-

---

[8] H. Rept. 113–481—*Department of Homeland Security Appropriations Bill, 2015.*
[9] *FirstLine Transportation Security Inc.* v. *United States,* 100 Fed Cl. 359 (2011).
[10] *Firstline Transportation Security, Inc* v. *U.S.* USCFC NO. 12–601 Nov 2012.
[11] Ibid.
[12] Ibid.

tion 15.308 when documenting its decisions in awarding four SPP contracts. Specifically, in this time period, TSA's documentation on proposal evaluations and decisions related to these contract awards was missing details and included inaccuracies. TSA did not formalize and implement procedures to ensure that SPP procurements were fully documented, and it did not have quality control procedures to verify the accuracy of data used for contract decisions. As a result, TSA risks not selecting the best contractor offer and not ensuring that it provides the best screening services. In four of the five procurement files for contracts awarded between January 2011 and August 2012, the rationale for TSA's final decisions on contractor selection was not fully described in supporting documentation."[13]

One troubling theme in TSA's SPP procurement process that was identified by the Court in the first rejected Kansas City award and is an issue in the second protest, is TSA's conduct of a "best value" analysis. As stated in the first Kansas City award protest ruling, in a "Best Value" determination a Government agency must compare the relative costs and benefits of the "competing proposals, including both price and non-price factors . . . "[14].

In the second RFP for Kansas City, TSA stated that "Security is paramount" and that "security is always TSA's most important objective" and that "security is a 'non-negotiable'" issue.[15] However, while not doubting the ability of the winning company to provide the level of screening services required by the contract, it is worth noting that both Kansas City awards went to the lowest bid. This is not surprising though given how TSA conduct its "best value" analysis. Obviously, if "security is paramount" and the "most important objective" one would think that a company's record of performance would be a considerable factor. However, in TSA's "best value analysis" price is the single most important factor. Price alone is equal to a combination of technical factors that include IN ORDER OF IMPORTANCE: (1) Operational Screening Management; (2) Program Management; (3) Logistics and Training; (4) Transition; and (5) Past Performance. So "Past Performance" is the least important factor in TSA's "security is the most important objective" best value analysis. In addition, while Factors 1 through 4 above are evaluated and provided an adjectival rating, past performance is rated on a pass/fail basis.[16]

It is understandable that "costs must be competitive" and the award cost-efficient for the Government. As discussed already and will be further discussed, ATSA requires private screeners to be no more expensive than the cost of Federal screeners, and so as threshold matter, in order for a company's bid to considered, it must be lower that than cost of using Federal screeners at the airport (which is the FCE). However, once it is determined that bidders are under the FCE, meaning they are less expensive than Federal screeners, and if "security is paramount" should price still trump all the technical factors combined? It goes without saying that it is in the public's best interest for TSA to properly award airport screening contracts using a true "best value" analysis which places a premium on performance capabilities as opposed making awards that are essentially (as Court decisions have shown) being made on a "low price technically acceptable" basis.

Other recent RFP issues include:

In the RFP for Sanford-Orlando 6 weeks after it was issued, TSA amended the solicitation to add over 10,000 hours for Behavior Detection Officer activities. However, in the Q&A for the solicitation, TSA stated that BDO activities were "not requirement of the contract." It is estimated that the additional BDO hours added would $15 million in contractor costs. Accordingly, it was expected that TSA would also adjust the maximum bid amount (the FCE) to reflect the added costs of the added BDO hours. However, in subsequent amendments to the RFP, TSA stated that the FCE would remain "unchanged" and then further explained "there is no change to the FCE is because the BDO level of effort is included in the original FCE as written in the Request for Proposal (RFP)."[17] That's some glaring omission!

TSA'S INTERPRETATION OF SPP SCREENER COMPENSATION REQUIREMENT UNDER ATSA

As noted in the introduction, ATSA requires that for a company to be "qualified to provide screening services," the company must "provide compensation and other benefits to such individuals that are not less than the level of compensation and

---

[13] DHS Office of Inspector General "TSA Screening Partnership Program" OIG–13–99 June 2013.

[14] See Footnote 9.

[15] *Airport Security Screening Services at MCI, Solicitation No. HST S05–12–R–SPP038* July 2012.

[16] Ibid. This evaluation analysis is the same in subsequent SPP solicitations.

[17] *Airport Security Screening Services at Orlando Sanford International Solicitation No. HSTS05–SPP004 Airport (SFB)*. See amendments 4, and 5.

other benefits provided to such Federal Government personnel." Accordingly, in SPP RFP's under the "Compensation and Benefits" clause TSA states that "TSA has interpreted the statute (ATSA) to require contract-screening companies to provide pay and benefits at a loaded cost (direct hour plus percentage cost of fringe benefits) to all screeners that equals or exceeds the loaded cost of the pay and benefits provided by the Federal Government. This approach: (1) Provides the contractor with flexibility to trade additional pay against other benefits, or to enhance certain benefits and reduce others; (2) enables the contractor to determine and provide the best package necessary for the recruitment and retention of quality private security screeners; and (3) increases flexibility while permitting recruitment and retention of quality private security screeners."[18] This interpretation seems plainly accurate—pay the same to screeners as would be provided by the Federal Government. It also recognizes the flexibility that the private sector has—which the Federal Government does not have—to balance wages and benefits to create a more a cost-efficient its labor force (which is discussed later).

However, TSA then says in the "Compensation and Benefits" clause "Therefore, the contractors shall provide at least the minimum loaded wage rate" (emphasis added).[19] Minimum screener rate? Yes. For all screeners? Yes. Regardless of the actual "level of compensation and other such benefits provided to such personnel?" Yes.

Under TSA's interpretation of the above ATSA language, all screeners, regardless of how long they have been on the job, can receive the "minimum rate" or starting TSO rate in a new SPP contract. Does TSA really believe that Congress intended, by using the phrase "not less than . . . such Federal Government personnel" to mean just not less than those TSA screeners who are making the minimum, starting TSO wage? So Congress intended that a screener with 12 years of experience could have his or her pay reduced to the starting screener wage whenever a private screening company took over screening at airport or when an existing SPP contract was re-awarded? Really?

In ATSA Congress mandated that the training of private screeners be equal to Federal screeners. Congress mandated that the level of screener performance be equal. And it seems logical and rational that Congress also mandated that the level of pay be equal. Yet, TSA believes Congress intended that the level of pay for private screeners, regardless of experience, only needs to be the "minimum rate." This seems quite illogical and irrational.

One would think in that given the legislative history and intent that sought to set up parallel/equivalent private and Federal screening forces that less than "such Federal Government personnel" clearly connotes parallel/equivalent pay for private and Federal screeners in the same situation or level of experience. In a job that supports an important homeland security mission and where "security is always TSA's most important objective" and "security is a 'non-negotiable'" TSA indeed seems to be negotiating away security with this screener pay requirement interpretation. Is this good public policy?

In other DHS agencies, such as the Federal Protective Service, where contract security personnel, like Federal and private airport screeners, are being successfully utilized to provide screening services and serve the Department's homeland security mission, when a new contractor takes over a contract the incumbent security officer wages cannot be reduced. Contractors receive seniority lists that let them know what they will have to pay in wages and benefits to the screening force. Obviously keeping wages stable promotes retention, retention of more experienced personnel, reduces turnover, and overall helps maintain or increase performance in their security mission. Conversely, if wages are cut it could promote instability, greater turnover, and the loss of experienced personnel. Again, aside from it being bad policy, a plain reading of the ATSA language and the intent behind that language, clearly does not support TSA's interpretation.

When asked about the issue of screeners having to take a pay cut with a new SPP contract, TSA stated that "TSA only monitors minimum salary requirements by means of the Compensation and Other Benefits clause in the SPP contracts. Actual salaries and wages for employees supporting a SPP contract are determined, as they are with all Federal contracts, by direct negotiation between the company and the employee. The Federal Government does not get involved in wages beyond ensuring that the compensation rate meets the requirements of the Aviation Transportation Security Act (Pub. L. 107–71)."[20]

---

[18] Ibid. See Clause H.6. Compensation and Other Benefits.
[19] Ibid.
[20] Responses to Screening Partnership Program (SPP) Questions for the Record Submitted by the House Committee on Appropriations Subcommittee on Homeland Security, March 25, 2014.

Obviously, a company can still submit a bid for an SPP contract that would pay screeners the equivalent of their Federal wages (with a new airport) or the equivalent of their current wages (with an existing SPP airport), and they are not required to bid starting screener wages. However, given that Price is the most important consideration that TSA uses in evaluating SPP bids, and the lowest bidders have been awarded the recent SPP contracts, for a screening company to submit a bid that provides "full pay"/"equivalent pay" seems to be a losing strategy.

By fostering a process where screeners, regardless of their experience/performance, must take a pay cut when an airport goes SPP or there is a new SPP contractor, TSA seems to have lost sight of its security mission. Are not airport screeners "front-line" homeland security personnel that play a vital role in transportation security? Does not TSA value the work of airport screeners? A forced pay cut will cause better performing and experienced screeners to leave and impact morale and could ultimately affect performance. In addition, no private company or the Federal Government has a surplus or alternative source of screeners so keeping incumbent screeners is vital and saves on training and hiring costs. Why is TSA trying to provide for security on the cheap at SPP airports?

If private screening companies, like contract security companies elsewhere in the Federal Government (and some companies are both), are required to bid equivalent wages and not minimum wages, and then such companies can beat the overall Federal screening cost number at an airport as required, how is this not: (1) What ATSA intended; (2) better for airports; (3) better for screeners; and (3) better for security? TSA and the Federal Government are still saving money!

THE FEDERAL COST ESTIMATE

TSA's definition and computation of the Federal Cost Estimate has been the subject of much inspection and investigation and is directly related to the "debate" as to whether the use of private screeners an airport is less expensive than using Federal screener. As noted above, the FCE was born out language in the 2012 FAA Modernization Act that amended ATSA and mandated that TSA approve an airport's SPP application, if "the Under Secretary determines that the approval would not compromise security or detrimentally affect the cost-efficiency or the effectiveness of the screening of passengers or property at the airport."[21] (Emphasis added). Accordingly, from a plain reading of the statutory language, the FCE represents the total Federal cost of using Federal screeners for "screening of passengers or property at the airport" and sets a maximum bid limit for private screening. It makes complete sense that if a private screening company bid for screening at the airport is not equal to or lower to the Federal costs, this would detrimentally affect the screening cost-efficiency at the airport which would violate ATSA and the bid should be considered unacceptable.

However, as is clearly apparent, and as TSA now readily admits, their computation of the FCE does not represent the complete/true cost of Federal screeners at an airport. It only represents an estimate of the costs to TSA, not the entire Federal Government (aka taxpayers). As stated by TSA, "In assessing cost-efficiency, TSA (only) compares costs within its appropriation to private-sector costs. While TSA computes imputed costs such as potential retirement it does not include those costs as part of its cost comparison for efficiency those prospective obligations are not are not provided in the agency's appropriation."[22]

Of course besides retirement, there are worker's compensation, legal, HR, administrative and other direct Federal (screener) costs being paid by taxpayers through other Federal agencies for "screening of passengers or property" at a Federalized airport. However, according to TSA's interpretation of the law, Congress intended "detrimentally affect cost-efficiency" to just apply to TSA's costs. For a short time, TSA could justify this interpretation of the law by referencing the Report accompanying the fiscal year 2013 Continuing Resolution where there was language that said TSA should not approve new contract applications if "the annual cost of the contract exceeds the annual cost to TSA of providing Federal screening services."[23] Unfortunately for TSA, Report language is not statutory language, that Report language expired after fiscal year 2013, and that language has been thoroughly reputed in subsequent Appropriations Reports.

In the Explanatory Statement for the fiscal year 2014 Consolidated Appropriations Act, TSA was directed "to implement generally accepted accounting methodolo-

---

[21] See Footnote 1.

[22] DHS Response to Questions from House Homeland Security Committee Chairman Michael McCaul, January 2014.

[23] Explanatory Statement accompanying *H.R. 933 Consolidated and Further Continuing Appropriations Act, 2013* see page S1552.

gies for cost and performance comparisons. As detailed in the House report, this includes, but is not limited to, comprehensive and accurate comparisons of Federal employee retirement costs and the administrative overhead associated with Federal screening services . . . With respect to TSA cost estimates, the study shall include indirect costs as recommended by GAO (GAO–09–27R)".[24]

This year the House's fiscal year 2015 DHS Appropriations Bill Report language is even more stern stating that TSA's use of an "FCE that utilizes faulty methodology and ignores significant costs to the Federal Government is unacceptable."[25] TSA also recently told the House Appropriations Committee in responses to questions on how TSA calculates its (TSA cost-only) FCE that "TSA is able to account for actual costs incurred for the majority of airport-specific costs." So what airport-specific costs are not being accounted for? And TSA said it is "confident the methodology is accurately capturing the most significant cost factors for Federal cost estimates." So what is not capturing or not accurately capturing?[26]

In TSA's last public iteration of a Federal-private cost comparison in 2011—which was done after numerous corrective recommendations by GAO—TSA alleged that private screeners were 3% more expensive. However, even after making numerous changes to its cost-methodology at the recommendation of GAO (which brought the TSA figure down from 17% to 9% to 3%) GAO still said of that comparison "we did not have confidence in the 3% figure because one of the issues that was still unresolved at that time was the question of uncertainty about the underlying estimate and the underlying assumptions going into the estimate."[27]

The DHS OIG has also found fault with TSA's cost comparisons. In a 2013 report on the SPP the OIG reviewed five contracts awarded between January 2011 and August 2012 for eight airport. The OIG office said "we reviewed two of eight cost estimates that TSA prepared for the five procurements and identified discrepancies in both cost estimates. Specifically, there were differences in labor hours and overtime rates. Inaccurate cost estimates could affect TSA's evaluation of offerors. A document included an incorrect figure, which resulted in a $162,057 overstatement of the cost to use private screeners. A document used to compare the estimated cost of private screening to the estimated cost of Federal screening showed TSA understated an estimate of the cost savings of private screening by $423,572."[28]

Given that TSA readily admits it does consider all the non-TSA costs associated with Federal screeners when it comes up with Federal screener cost estimates, and given the lack of confidence and accuracy even in those costs, and given the lack of confidence in TSA's cost-comparison methodology, it is really disingenuous to say that TSA has found the cost of private screeners to be more expensive that Federal screeners. And, even with TSA only using an incomplete TSA-only FCE, that may or may not even capture or capture accurately the TSA airport-specific costs, because of the many cost-efficient and cost-saving policies and practices that private screening companies utilize, private screening companies are still able to beat the TSA's incomplete FCE in SPP RFP's!

WHY PRIVATE SCREENING COMPANIES ARE MORE COST-EFFICIENT THAN THE FEDERAL GOVERNMENT IN PROVIDING AIRPORT SCREENING

Even paying the same (equivalent) wages, private companies can beat the total cost of screening relative to TSA's actual costs, and of course, relative to total Federal costs. There are many reasons for this greater cost-efficiency. First as mentioned above, TSA allows contractors to provide pay and benefits at a loaded cost (direct hour plus percentage cost of fringe benefits) and as TSA admits "This approach: (1) provides the contractor with flexibility to trade additional pay against other benefits . . . that enables the contractor to determine and provide the best package necessary for the recruitment and retention of quality private security

---

[24] Explanatory Statement on *H.R. 3547, Consolidated Appropriations Act, 2014*, See Page H932.

[25] *House Report 113–481—DEPARTMENT OF HOMELAND SECURITY APPROPRIATIONS BILL, 2015*—Privatized Screening. "Further, the Committee remains concerned with TSA's use, as it is currently construed, of a Federal Cost Estimate (FCE). Using a FCE that utilizes faulty methodology and ignores significant costs to the Federal Government is unacceptable. The Committee expects TSA to implement generally accepted accounting methodologies for cost and performance comparisons, as described in Public Law 113–76, which includes, but is not limited to, proper, comprehensive, and accurate comparisons of Federal employee retirement costs and the administrative overhead associated with Federal screening services."

[26] See Footnote 20.

[27] Ms. Jennifer Grover, Homeland Security and Justice, Response to a question at the January 14, 2014 Hearing of the Committee on Government Reform Subcommittee on Government Operations "TSA Oversight: Examining the Screening Partnership Program. (See Footnote 2).

[28] See Footnote 13.

screeners."[29] Through this flexibility on balancing wages and benefits, which the Federal Government does not have with TSA screeners, contractors are able to create incentives and disincentives for its workers that result in better attendance, timeliness, performance which all can save money. Take sick leave. When a screener calls in sick the usual response is to have to pay another screener overtime to cover the shift. It can also lead to lanes being opened late. To reduce such incidents private companies can trade sick leave for increased wages. There are other ways too for private employers to balance wages and benefits that will increase cost-efficiency.

Another area where cost-efficiencies can be realized is by reducing absenteeism. In a 2013 GAO Report on screener misconduct, of the 9,600 cases of employee misconduct investigated and adjudicated from fiscal years 2010 through 2012, the No. 1 category that accounted for 32 percent of the cases was attendance and leave-related misconduct.[30] This backed up a 2011 OPM finding that "Attendance issues are among the most common challenges for Federal supervisors." The OPM report noted that "Employees' failure to report to work as scheduled can have a negative impact on an organization's ability to complete the mission." (What is interesting is that there is no mention in the Report of any "negative impact" of additional costs associated with Federal employee absenteeism.)

As private screening companies have to pay for absenteeism out of their set contract amount they are very motivated prevent and discourage absenteeism. As such, bonuses are provided for perfect attendance and robust attendance policies are maintained. There is little doubt that the punishment for an unexcused absence is greater in the private sector than in the Federal sector. In addition, not only does absenteeism cost money, but just one late screener can prevent the "critical mass" needed to open a check point which affects performance. If during the "morning rush" at airport there are screening lanes not being used, it is probably a result of an unexcused or excused (call in sick) absence.

Another significant cost driver is injury rates and workers compensation claims. While TSA does not bear the full cost of paying Federal screener worker compensation claims, and has no incentive to reduce or question those claims, again, it is the opposite with private screening companies. Again, SPP companies must pay for all their screener worker's compensation claims out of the fixed contract amount. Accordingly, SPP companies employ a variety of methods to reduce, mitigate, manage, and limit worker compensation claims. Companies use pre-hire physical testing protocols coupled with other at-work initiatives that minimize on-the-job injuries, and allow for faster return to work and lower workers compensation rates.

To address widespread baggage screener injuries, one SPP company created a non-certified position assigned only to lift bags for the certified baggage screeners (significantly reducing screener injuries and workers compensation costs). At a Federalized airport a new OPM job classification would first be required for a solution. SPP companies also employ full-time health and safety professionals on site to investigate and study injuries and devise ways to mitigate them.

Reducing attrition is another way to save money. In terms of hiring and retention of screeners, SPP companies do many things that TSA does not or cannot do. In hiring screeners, SPP companies do their own local recruiting and screen applicants before submitting them for the formal TSA screening process. Even after a prospective screener passes the TSA screening process, he or she can still go through a company interview with supervisors before being hired. SPP companies will also provide monetary and other incentives to retain screeners. At airports using Federal screeners, screeners can show up for work, sight unseen already hired. The additional steps that SPP companies apply to the recruitment process results in more successful new hire completion rates and on-going on-the-job success. SPP companies fully realize that a stable workforce is more efficient, effective, and motivated. In the 2011 Report by the House Transportation and Infrastructure Committee on the SPP, it was calculated that the turnover rate at the non-SPP LAX airport was 13.8% compared to 8.7% at the SPP San Francisco (SFO) airport.[31]

How does TSA stack up with SPP companies in the areas of attrition, absenteeism and injury rates? As GAO reported at the January 2014 OGR GO Subcommittee hearing on the SPP it found out while doing its 2012 Report comparing Federal and private screener performance, that even though contractors collect and report this information to the SPP PMO, the TSA Office of Human Capital does not collect the data and TSA does not require contractors to use the same human capital metrics

[29] See Footnotes 17 and 18.
[30] GAO, TRANSPORTATION SECURITY.—TSA Could Strengthen Monitoring of Allegations of Employee Misconduct, GAO–13–624, July 2013.
[31] See Footnote 5.

as TSA, and comparisons are not conducted.[32] In a follow-up to this finding, in a question for the record of the hearing, the Ranking Member of the subcommittee, Gerry Connolly the DHS OIG if TSA planned to collect this data "in a consistent manner so that comparisons can be made between airports?" The Response was "Cost and screening performance are the two areas where the Transportation Security Administration (TSA) compares the Screening Partnership Program (SPP) airports and non-SPP airports. Metrics such as attrition, absenteeism, or injury rates are not included as germane to the definitions of either cost or screening performance and, thus, are not monitored on a consistent basis."[33] Maybe they should be. These human capital measures are huge cost factors and a measure of an efficient and effective workforce.

A major cost-saving advantage that SPP companies have over TSA is in scheduling and managing its screener force which creates cost savings compared to Federal screening. At Federally-screened airports, the number of full-time and part-time screeners (actually FTE's) is dictated to TSA airport directors by TSA headquarters. At SPP airports, the SPP company site manager can schedule screeners as needed in order to meet the contract requirement for total screener hours. As stated in SPP RFP's "The Contractor shall schedule their workforce in a manner that meets demands for security screening and work closely with TSA staff to satisfy all operational requirements in the contract."[34] This scheduling flexibility results in numerous cost efficiencies. For instance, at most larger airports, the terminals are open for 20 hours. Under TSA's staffing model, this would require two full-time screeners at 8 hours per shift and one part-time screener for 4 hours to staff the position, with all three screeners receiving fixed benefits. On the other hand, at one SPP airport with such terminal operating hours, the SPP company is able to schedule two screeners at two 10-hour shifts reducing personnel and costs. TSA does not utilize such an option. SPP companies also take steps that TSA does not to schedule breaks and "relief" more cost-efficiently.

SPP companies also use sophisticated airline industry-based scheduling tools, which further efficiently schedule and manage staffing in real time. In making their screening schedules companies can make pinpoint adjustments using optimization software and airline data. They have decision support systems that allow managers to be proactive. Scheduling is also tied in directly with payroll, HR, and training systems, which ensure full visibility of manpower resources. For TSA, effective and efficient scheduling is a problem due to centralization of the scheduling system and institutional inflexibility. In 2008, the DHS Office of Inspector General found that "TSA is overly reliant on the (National mobile) deployment force to fill chronic staffing shortages at specific airports in lieu of more cost effective strategies and solutions to handle screening demands."[35]

All the above-mentioned cost-efficiency activities—reducing "sick leave", reducing attendance/absentee rates, reducing and mitigating injuries, efficient scheduling as well as efficient use of part-time screeners—also all contribute to one of the greatest cost-savers: Reducing screener overtime. Overtime costs are huge and it would great to see an apples-to-apples comparison of TSA and SPP overtime costs.

While personnel and compensation costs represent by far the largest screening cost area, and as discussed private companies are finding cost efficiencies in this area, the largest relative cost-efficiencies for the private sector over the Federal sector is in administration and management functions that are not screener functions/ positions. This includes recruiting, on-boarding, certain training, administration of payroll, administration of workplace injuries, administration of HR-related employment matters (a big area), benefits administration, labor relations, quality control inspections, staffing management, IT support, accounting and budget management, and many more. While TSA (and other Federal agencies supporting Federal screener) also do these tasks, private companies are more experienced and motivated to save costs in these areas and, like with scheduling, they utilize the most efficient methods, technologies, and staff to accomplish these tasks. In addition, private companies control the compensation paid to its administrators. Also, the private sector is more cost-efficient in handling legal settlements and disputes (as well as workplace injuries as mentioned above). In April of this year, TSA just settled a case that started in 2010 involving the harassment and humiliation of a woman who, in accordance with TSA guidelines asked that her breast milk not be X-rayed, but instead on two successive occasions was harassed and humiliated by TSA screeners.

---

[32] Testimony of Jennifer Grover. See Footnote 2.
[33] Question for the Record. See Footnote 2 (Page 65).
[34] See Footnote 17. Clause C.4.2.3 Scheduling.
[35] DHS Office of Inspector General, *The Transportation Security Administration's National Deployment Force* (April 2008) (OIG–08–49).

It cost the Federal Government $75,000 and who know how many hours of legal work.[36]

What motivates private companies to find cost efficiencies in their screening operations and administration? First, constant competition from other contractors forces companies to perform well, employ best practices, reduce waste, and seek to constantly improve. Second, there is profit. And if screening companies can, as required by ATSA, "provide a level of screening services and protection equal to or greater" than TSA screeners using private screeners "who meet all the requirements . . . applicable to" TSA screeners, and at the same time make a profit, then what is the problem?

In addition, while seeking to find cost efficiencies in operations and administration is one way to earn a profit, another way is through better performance. At SPP airports, the screening operation is indeed a business, and better performance is good for business both tangibly (award fees) and intangibly (reputation and future business). SPP company site mangers are very vested in hiring the right people, monitoring performance, and striving for better-than-average performance. Bonuses are provided based on merit, not simply seniority. Employees are well aware that if they do not perform they could be out of a job and a culture of cohesion and teamwork within the workforce and peer expectations are encouraged. These employee performance and cost-containment drivers (especially in the areas of absenteeism and overtime as mentioned above) are not present in the Federal sector and DHS (and TSA) are beset with its own host of employee performance and motivation issues.[37] At Federal airports, TSA headquarters sets compensation for screeners and managers and screeners have no real financial incentives to perform beyond the minimum requirements and barring the commission of a crime or serious violation of standards, Federal screeners and managers—like all Federal workers—have great job security.[38]

TSA SHOULD NOT BE BOTH THE REGULATOR AND OPERATOR OF AIRPORT SCREENING

One of the SPP's Guiding Principles is to "Create a partnership that leverages strengths of the private and public sectors: TSA believes the SPP can only achieve its objectives if contract operators and TSA work in close partnership, leveraging private sector innovations and efficiencies with Government security oversight."[39] Amen. Such a cost-efficient partnership is how screening is conducted at virtually every other industrialized/Western nation in the world. As documented in the House T&I SPP Report, in other countries where the danger of aviation terrorism is equally of great National concern "Federal oversight of qualified private contract screeners has shown to be effective all over the world (and) almost all Western countries operate civil aviation security through the use of Federal oversight of private contract screeners. Other than Romania, Poland, and Bulgaria, the United States has the only Government in the Western world that functions as the airport security operator, administrator, regulator, and auditor."[40]

There are sound policy and operational reasons for not wanting TSA to be both the regulator and operator of airport screening. First, the enormous task of managing the 55,000 or more TSA employees involved in airport screening diverts and denigrates TSA's ability to focus on critical transportation security-related functions such as setting security standards, technology adoption, conducting risk management analyses, performing oversight, enforcing standards and regulations, analyzing intelligence, auditing screening operations, and doing more to stop aviation-related terror before the terrorists get to the airport. Second, as the entity both conducting the screening and overseeing the screening, there are inherently greater risks of poor screener performance going uncorrected or even worse being encouraged or covered up by management.

---

[36] http://www.dailybreeze.com/general-news/20140422/hermosa-beach-mom-wins-settlement-from-tsa-over-airport-breast-feeding-incident.

[37] In the December 2013 OPM Survey DHS ranked tied for the worst out of 37 Federal agencies in "Intrinsic Work Experience" which reflects the employees' feelings of motivation and competency relating to their role in the workplace. *2013 Federal Employee Viewpoint Survey Results; Employees Influencing Change; Governmentwide Management Report United States Office of Personnel Management* In a December 2012 Merit Systems Protection Board Report, DHS ranked tied for 23rd out of 25 agencies in an employee motivation survey. *Federal Employee Engagement: The Motivating Potential of Job Characteristics and Rewards.* A Report to the President and the Congress of the United States by the U.S. Merit Systems Protection Board, December 2012.

[38] Dennis Cauchon "Some federal workers more likely to die than lose jobs" *USA TODAY*, July 19, 2011.

[39] See Footnote 17. Orlando-Sanford RFP. Section C—Statement of Work, C.1 Introduction.

[40] See Footnote 6.

In 2011, this latter concern came to full fruition where an investigation at Hawaii's Honolulu International Airport uncovered a massive on-going security breach involving improper (lack of) screening of checked bags for explosives. About TSA workers at the airport were fired and another 15 suspended including screeners, their supervisors, and the Federal Security Director. The TSA screeners claimed they were forced to abandon required screening practices because of TSA management pressure.[41] Could TSA managers at an SPP airport, operating at "arm's length", be able to pressure a private screening company to abandon required screening practices putting the company in clear default of its entire contract? Not likely. The potential loss of a contract and hundreds of jobs is a strong incentive for a company, and everyone in the company, to make sure that all employees are compliant with the requirements of the contract. At the Hawaii airport, the malfeasant Federal screeners, managers, and security director were simply replaced by other Federal employees.

TSA can and does provide effective oversight of private screening services. Among the tools that TSA uses to track screener performance are daily TSA manager reports, monthly Performance Management Reviews calculated against challenging metrics, and twice-yearly award fee reviews also calculated against challenging performance metrics. TSA can be assured, and indeed constantly assures itself, that SPP companies perform at a very high level.

FEDERAL V. PRIVATE SCREENER PERFORMANCE COMPARISONS

As to the issue of accurate performance comparisons between Federal screeners and private screeners, as noted earlier this year by GAO at a House Oversight Subcommittee hearing, GAO said that when it did its 2012 report on screener performance, it found that "while TSA had conducted prior reports commissioned prior reports comparing the performance of SPP and non-SPP airports, TSA officials stated at the time that they did not plan to conduct similar analyses in the future.[42] Also, for the screener performance data that GAO analyzed, while they found that there were differences in performance between SPP and non-SPP airports, and those differences could not be exclusively attributed to the use of either Federal or private screeners."[43] Not particularly helpful.

GAO recommended that TSA develop a mechanism to develop to regularly monitor private versus Federal screener performance and TSA concurred with the recommendation. As a result, GAO reported at the January 2014 hearing, in January 2013, TSA issued its first SPP Annual Report covering fiscal year 2012, which "compares the performance of SPP airports with the average performance of airports in their respective category, as well as the average performance for all airports, for three performance measures: TIP detection rates, recertification pass rates, and PACE evaluation results."[44] However, GAO did not elaborate on the performance comparisons (either the accuracy or results) nor is the SPP Annual Report in the public domain.

The lack of comparable performance or TSA's reluctance to share performance data that it considers to Sensitive Security Information (SSI) hinders the SPP. SPP companies believe that they would compare quite favorably in the major performance metric with Federal screeners. Airports interested in the SPP should be able to see the performance data of SPP airports and TSA should share its monthly Office of Security Operations Executive Scorecard with airport directors.

While the level of communication between SPP companies and local TSA officials, program managers, and contracting officials remains high, the flow of information from TSA headquarters to screening companies, and airports, has diminished. The ability for the screening companies, airports, and TSA to work together has been limited by a lack of TSA sharing of important performance and service data and the agency often taking a "my way or the highway approach" to doing things. In addition, as TSA has become more secretive and guarded with its information, a few years ago TSA also took a significant step to limit the ability of SPP companies to share information. In SPP contracts there is now a clause that prohibits the SPP company from publicly disseminating "publicity releases . . . in connection with or referring to the contract" or "any information, oral or written, concerning the results or conclusions made pursuant to the performance" of the contract "without prior

---

[41] *http://www.hawaiinewsnow.com/story/19778673/homeland-security-probes-unscreened-bags-in-hawaii.*
[42] Testimony of Jennifer Grover at January 2014 OGR GO SC hearing referring to GAO Report "SCREENING PARTNERSHIP PROGRAM: TSA Should Issue More Guidance to Airports and Monitor Private versus Federal Screener Performance" December 2012, GAO–13–208.
[43] Ibid.
[44] Ibid.

written consent of the Contracting Officer."[45] This includes seminars, professional society meeting/conferences and even requests for information from Congress. Before this "gag order" was put in place, SPP companies were already prohibited from releasing protected Government information under both previous contract language and various Federal laws. Given the broadness of this clause, SPP companies are now reticent to discuss almost any aspect of their performance—including those type of "good news" screener stories that TSA likes to publicize about Federal screeners—with anyone without first receiving TSA's written permission. This could severely restrict the amount of information available to airports, Congress, and the public about the SPP.

Better performance comparisons though could be on the way. In the Report accompanying the fiscal year 2014 Consolidated Appropriations Act, "TSA is directed to allocate resources for an independent study of the performance of Federalized compared to privatized screening. The study shall include, but not be limited to, security effectiveness, cost, throughput, wait times, management efficiencies, and customer satisfaction."[46] As mentioned above, TSA was also directed to "implement generally accepted accounting methodologies" for its own future cost and performance comparison, and also to implement past GAO recommendations for comparing cost and performance. Of course, whether TSA makes the relevant data available to the study investigators, whether such data is accurate, whether such data is comparable, and then in what form the results can be provided remain to be seen.

The "customer satisfaction" comparisons should be quite interesting. SPP companies realize the value of customer service and they teach and reinforce customer service constantly. Treating passengers politely is not only the right thing to do, but avoiding incidents and maintaining a calmer passenger base makes it easier for screeners and behavior detection officers to spot aberrant behavior. Even with the difficult protocols, SPP screeners are taught to implement them with customer service empathy. It is no surprise that Kansas City International Airport, an SPP location earned the J.D. Power and Associates award for highest customer satisfaction of all medium-sized North American airports twice in recent years. That airport's screening services as well as other SPP companies have garnered much praise from their airport directors for customer service and other innovations that have improved screening operations.[47] For those airports wanting to join the SPP, greater customer service and greater accountability are major reasons. Said one airport official whose airport had applied to the SPP, "As we have documented, TSA employees frequently have no concern for customer service. We feel that participating in the SPP will increase screening efficiency and flexibility and improve the customer service experience."[48]

At the January 2014 House hearing on the SPP, TSA was sharply criticized for the continuing customer service failures of TSA officers. Ranking Dem Jerry Connelly, in recounting an incident he saw involving a Federal screener stated that "there is no excuse that someone barking orders continuously at the public at any airport in America who is an employee of Federal Government . . . I'd lose my job if I treated the public that way. And rightfully so. My staff would be fired if I find that they treated my public that way. And we need to hold ourselves to that standard. And so, I fear it's beyond anecdotal."[49]

CONCLUSION

Many airports are satisfied with their Federal screening force and the ATSA language establishing the SPP in no way pushes or even encourages airports to use private screening companies. However, it is clear that Congress wanted airports to at least have a fair opportunity to utilize private screening which by law has to be equal to or greater in the level of security provided. From the experiences and lessons learned in the SPP, and when considering a true cost comparison it is clear that the use of private screening companies is viable and effective option for airports, and a cost-efficient option for TSA and the Federal Government. As TSA states, the SPP is about "leveraging private sector innovations and efficiencies with Government security oversight."[50]

However, TSA's very questionable interpretations of SPP statutes, its faulty RFP and award process, as well as other actions related to the SPP is threatening the

---

[45] TSA Clause H.5200.205.001 "Publicity and Dissemination of Contract Information".
[46] See Footnote 24.
[47] See Footnote 5. T&I SPP Report. Appendix 12 SPP Testimonials.
[48] See Footnote 5. May 20, 2011 Letter to House T&I Committee from Springfield-Branson National Airport.
[49] See Footnote 2.
[50] See Footnote 39.

viability of program. While TSA's refusal to use a Federal cost estimate that reflects the true cost to the Federal Government is makes for an unfair comparison between Federal and private screener costs and seems to go against ATSA, it is understandable that TSA would not like to spend more of its budget on private screeners than it spends on Federal screeners. However, even with a TSA cost-only FCE, private screening companies, because of greater flexibility and other cost-efficient reasons, can beat a TSA cost-only Federal screening estimate. They can also beat the TSA cost-only price if they have to pay screeners "equivalent" wages. Yet TSA's dubious belief that ATSA only requires private screening companies to bid (pay) minimum TSA screener wages, and TSA's focus on price in its "best value" award analyzes, is setting up a situation that will effectively mean every time an SPP contract awarded, screeners will take a pay cut. This seems completely incongruous with the mission of maintaining an effective screening force, it flies in the face of how contract security personnel are treated by other DHS agencies, and it will only create dissatisfied screeners and airports.

It is therefore unfortunate and indeed ironic that at a time with unprecedented interest and emphasis on Government efficiency and sustained and meaningful private-sector job growth, the TSA is choking a successful public-private partnership program that is exceedingly efficient, effective, and customer-focused. Far from ignoring the SPP, in its mission to provide the best possible aviation security, the TSA should be embracing it.

Mr. HUDSON. Thank you, Mr. Amitay.
The Chairman will recognize Mr. Cox to testify.

STATEMENT OF J. DAVID COX, SR., NATIONAL PRESIDENT, AMERICAN FEDERATION OF GOVERNMENT EMPLOYEES

Mr. COX. Mr. Chairman, Members of the subcommittee, thank you for the opportunity to testify today.

It is clear that the Screening Partnership Program, SPP, does not improve aviation security and it does not save the taxpayers money. Rather, SPP harms security, costs more, and hurts the TSOs who bear the brunt of the outsourcing program. Only security contractors benefit.

There is no demand for airports to privatize the work of our Nation's TSOs. Although the 2012 FAA Modernization and Reform Act made it easy for airports to apply to privatize their TSA workforce, only a handful have done so. With the exception of the Montana airports, over the past 2 years, only three airports have asked TSA for permission to switch to private screeners.

But that legislation left intact the requirement that SPP contractors provide private screeners compensation and other benefits that are not less than the level of compensation and other benefits provided to TSOs. AFGE members at the four Montana airports currently transitioning from Federal to private have informed us this is definitely not the case.

The right of first refusal for a job with a private contractor is not meaningful because, in Montana, it means a significant cut in pay, benefits, and career development opportunities. Even though CSSI FirstLine, the Montana contractor, has promised to match TSOs' current pay, many have chosen to uproot their lives and families to transfer to other Federal airports, retire far earlier than they had planned, or simply leave TSA rather than work for peanuts for the contractor.

AFGE has confirmed that the benefits offered by FirstLine are not equivalent to those provided by TSA.

The health insurance plan offered by the contractor is a high-deductible health reimbursement account whose in-network providers are in Tennessee, approximately 1,800 miles from Montana. There are no in-State providers under the plan.

Premiums are higher and benefits are woefully inferior. TSA offers 11 Nation-wide plans and 2 specific to Montana, and even the most bare bones of these is far more generous to employees than the contractor plan.

Other than vague statements that they are working on future pension benefit, FirstLine offers no retirement benefit, no defined benefit pension, no 401(k) savings plan, no profit-sharing plan, no IRA, no employee stock ownership plan, nothing. In short, FirstLine refuses to make even the smallest gesture toward benefit equivalency that the statute demands.

AFGE strongly supports the Contract Screener Reform and Accountability Act introduced by Ranking Member Bennie Thompson and Representative Sheila Jackson Lee and Nita Lowey, long-standing champions of our Nation's security and the TSO workforce. Mr. Chairman, the TSOs' voices should not be lost in this committee's discussion about SPP.

I would like to conclude my testimony by reading to you an excerpt from an e-mail from one of our Montana TSO members.

"After 9/11, I wanted to do something to ensure that that horror would never be repeated. So I became a screener at the Bozeman airport in Montana.

"The SPP program leaves very little for a person of my age. At age 58 and with almost 12 years of service with TSA, I will be left with very little to show for it.

"When I looked into working for the private company, I learned that FirstLine provides no retirement plan. I was told that that would be up to me personally, no plan and no match by the company. This is not comparable to TSA.

"Health benefits have decreased in a major way. FirstLine's medical plan has an $8,000 deductible for a single person and $11,000 deductible for a family. This deductible would have to be met before any health care expenses would be covered. This is not comparable to TSA.

"Transfer opportunities to other airports were limited, but after living here since 1993, it is not a viable option. Either my husband would have to leave his job of over 21 years or I would have to leave my home and family.

"I am just a little old lady who has worked her entire life to ensure the wellbeing of others. I believe I deserve better from this from TSA."

Mr. Chairman, I would really like to thank the subcommittee for the opportunity to represent the TSO workforce at this important hearing, and I would be happy to answer any questions.

[The prepared statement of Mr. Cox follows:]

PREPARED STATEMENT OF J. DAVID COX, SR.

JULY 29, 2014

Mr. Chairman, Ranking Member Richmond, and Members of the subcommittee: My name is J. David Cox, Sr., and I am the national president of the American Federation of Government Employees, AFL–CIO (AFGE). On behalf of the more than 670,000 Federal and District of Columbia workers our union represents, including 45,000 Transportation Security Officers (TSOs) working to provide safe and secure travel for over 2 million passengers each day, I thank you for the opportunity to testify today on the hearing entitled "Examining TSA's Management of the Screening Partnership Program (SPP)."

Oversight of TSA's management of the SPP must extend beyond the ease with which contractors are approved for SPP contracts. It must also include a close examination of the effect of the program on aviation security and the TSO workforce. TSA SPP FAQs clearly state that "Federal and privatized screening have comparable performance, and there is no measurement indicating there is a difference in customer service." SPP decisions are not based on TSO performance at a given airport. Private screeners follow the same standard operating procedures and use the same equipment as Federal TSOs. The only difference is that after privatization, the TSOs risk replacement by workers lacking their training and on-the-job experience while all Federal TSA management remains on the job. SPP does not exist to further aviation security or save taxpayer money. TSOs, the front line of aviation security, bear the brunt of an outsourcing program that benefits no party involved except security contractors.

BACKGROUND

In the aftermath of the terrible events of September 11, 2001, Congress quickly enacted the Aviation and Transportation Security Act (ATSA) to correct the gaping holes in our Nation's security net made apparent by the ability of the 9/11 hijackers to hijack planes in a coordinated attack that killed over 2,900 people, and injured more than 6,700. Although al-Qaeda's violent, irrational hatred for the United States was the root cause of the 9/11 tragedy, Congress pinpointed the lack of a well-trained, experienced screening workforce receiving adequate pay and benefits as one of the underlying issues that left our country vulnerable to the worst act of aviation terrorism in history. To resolve that issue, Congress Federalized screening duties in ATSA, with the belief that improved training, pay, benefits, and working conditions would lead to a stable workforce focused on security. TSA, according to a March 30, 2005, Congressional Research Service report, was given "direct responsibility for passenger screening." The TSO workforce AFGE represents proves every day that Congress made the right decision in Federalizing screening duties.

The SPP runs counter to the National consensus that the screening of passengers and baggage at our Nation's airports should be performed by Federal employees to tighten the aviation security safety net. There is no documentation of the superiority of private screeners to TSOs. There are no cost savings. Airports seeking to escape TSA management through SPP risk losing an experienced and trained screening workforce, yet they will retain every single layer of expensive TSA management. TSA's cost comparison analysis is opaque at best. Indeed, the current SPP upends the lives and careers of an airport's TSO workforce, leave the traveling public no safer, and provides no taxpayer savings.

It is important to note that changes to the SPP included in the FAA Modernization and Reform Act of 2012 were never subject to the Congressional debate and scrutiny applied to the decision to Federalize aviation security. The provisions of the FAA Modernization and Reform Act are so broad and so biased in favor of privatization that it could unravel the aviation security safety net our country has worked so hard to achieve if not modified by Congress.

THERE IS NO DEMAND FOR SPP

First, only 18 of the Nation's 457 commercial airports have private-sector security screeners. That's less than 4 percent. Except for San Francisco and four other airports that were part of the initial SPP pilot program (Kansas City International Airport, Greater Rochester International Airport, Jackson Hole Airport, and Tupelo Regional Airport), the only airports to seek privatization have been small airports in Iowa, New Mexico, Montana, Florida, and New Hampshire. A representative hearing on SPP would include the directors of our airports in New York, Chicago, Los Angeles, Miami, Denver, Atlanta, Washington, DC, and every other major gateway that have chosen to work with TSA and its National network of highly-qualified TSOs. None of these airports has shown the slightest interest in privatization, yet none is ever heard from in these hearings.

Second, despite legislation passed in 2012 making it easier for airports to apply to privatize their TSA workforce, only a handful of airports have applied to do so. Aside from Montana, over the last 2 years, only three airports—the small Orlando-Sanford and Sarasota Bradenton airports in Florida and the airport in Portsmouth, NH, have asked TSA for permission to make the switch to private screeners. The lack of interest was noted by the GAO in December 2012. "Airport operators from 3 airports that have not applied to the SPP expressed no interest in the SPP, and stated that they are generally satisfied with the level of screening service provided by TSA," GAO said.

Third, when larger airports consider SPP and then learn the facts, they stick with the TSOs. In 2013, the elected managers of Sacramento International Airport agreed to consider a proposal by their airport director to join SPP. But when they studied the facts of the situation, and how it would affect their local screeners, the Sacramento Board of Supervisors reversed its earlier decision and voted by a wide margin against TSA privatization. One of the factors they considered in Sacramento was precedent: No airport that large has made the switch from public to private. Four small airports have made the switch; but of these, only two, Roswell, NM, and Sioux Falls, IA, actually "opted out" of TSA and joined SPP on their own. Roswell did so because it wanted to hire locals at its remote location in eastern New Mexico. Sioux Falls, according to a 2010 staff report prepared for the Colorado Springs, CO, airport, had a director with an "an anti-Federal Government ideology" who was "looking for ways to keep Federal screeners out of his airport." The other two airports that moved from TSA to a private screener, Marathon, FL, and Sonoma, CA, did so at the suggestion of TSA during the Bush administration. It's very clear from this history that there is simply no demand from the airport community at large to privatize the operations of the TSA, period.

So where does the interest come from? It's striking how little the privatizers actually talk about security in their public discussion of the issues. Companies like Firstline constantly talk about how SPP provides them with "flexibility" to move employees around, but never discuss the task of securing the American flying public. That's because they are interested in profit, not security. And how do they make that profit? They make it by paying lower wages and providing fewer and less comprehensive benefits, such as health insurance and pensions. That does nothing but line the pockets of contractors and deprives airport security screeners of the living standards and financial security they deserve.

Despite the fact that security is not improved by going private, the Federal Government and U.S. taxpayers are forced to bear the costs of any airport that shifts from Federal to private. Airports with a troubled relationship with TSA find little resolution to their problem by applying to SPP: The same TSA management, policies, and procedures remain after privatization. The only new factor is a very inexperienced workforce of private screeners.

SPP LEAVES THE TSO WORKFORCE IN A "NO WIN" SITUATION WITH FEW GOOD ALTERNATIVES

TSA accepted the joint bid of CSSI/Firstline Security to provide private screening at Bozeman, Bert Mooney, Glacier Park International, and Yellowstone airports in Montana. Despite the security issues that arise from the State's status as a border State, most of the commercial air traffic in Montana is subject to private screening under the SPP. The transition to SPP at the four Montana airports has provided AFGE a clear view of the impact of privatization on incumbent TSOs at privatized airports, as well as the workers contractors hire "off the street" to work at those airports. It is important to note that SPP contractors can only make a profit by manipulating the payroll. Federal law requires SPP contractors to provide "compensation and other benefits" to their employees "that are not less than the level of compensation and other benefits provided" to TSOs. AFGE has documented that this is simply not the case in Montana and we have reason to believe it is not the case at other SPP airports around the country.

Our union has opposed the SPP since its inception. It is inconsistent with ATSA's goal of Federalizing the process of screening passengers and baggage. TSA has approved bids from contractors that provide substantially lower pay and benefits those received by TSOs. It also allows SPP contractors to deviate from the Staffing Allocation Model (SAM) that applies to Federal airports. It is AFGE's position that security contractors would be unable to show the "cost efficiencies" required under the law, if not for TSA's permissive allowance for lower pay, benefits that shift the cost to worker or are virtually non-existent, and a lack of compliance with the SAM. The table will be set for aviation security to devolve to pre-September 11 levels because the low pay and benefits will drive private screeners to leave the security contractor for better-paying jobs with better benefits.

Union members in Montana have informed us that CSSI/Firstline is offering new hires starting salaries that are thousands of dollars lower than TSA's starting rates, and that with regard to "paid time off," the contractor's allowances are drastically inferior to what is provided to TSOs and other Federal employees. Federal employees with up to 3 years of service earn 13 days of annual leave a year and 9 days of sick leave. The contractor offers just 12 days total of combined "paid time off

(PTO)" for employees for the first 5 years of service. Federal employees with more than 3 years but less than 15 years of service earn 20 days of annual leave per year, and 9 days of sick leave. The contractor provides 18 days of combined PTO for employees with between 6 and 10 years of service. Federal employees and TSOs with 15 or more years of service earn 26 days of annual leave and 9 days of sick leave; in contrast, the contractor offers a total of 19 days of combined PTO for employees with 11 or more years of service.

Importantly, Federal TSOs and other Federal employees are given credit for years of honorable military service in calculating their eligibility for annual leave accrual. Thus, a TSO who has served his country in the armed services for any amount of time (including both active duty and active duty for training) will earn annual leave according to tenure with includes his time served in the military. Agencies also have the flexibility to provide service credit for prior non-Federal/non-military service when determining a new employee's annual leave accrual rates. This is an important management flexibility that assists in recruitment, given the fact that Federal salaries lag those in the private sector.

Federal TSOs are also eligible for leave sharing, leave transfer, and carrying over up to 30 days of paid time off. They receive paid "administrative" time off to serve on a jury or to be a witness in a legal proceeding. Federal employees are also entitled to take up to 3 days of funeral leave to arrange or attend the funeral of a close relative who dies as a result of military service in a combat zone.

The health insurance benefit being offered by the contractor is almost laughable as health insurance, but there is nothing funny about how inferior it is to FEHBP's plans. Its value to the employee is far below that of any of the 11 Nation-wide plans currently available to TSOs in Montana, even the one "high deductible" plan from GEHA. The contractor's plan is a high-deductible Health Reimbursement Account plan, a type that is inferior even to the Health Savings Account Plans available in the Federal Employees Health Benefits Program (FEHBP). And to make matters worse, the contractor's plan's "network" of providers are all in the State of Tennessee, approximately 1,800 miles from Montana. Thus, participants would effectively be denied access to the plan's network, and thereby be forced to pay the higher, out-of-network costs unless they happened to be vacationing in Tennessee when a need for health care arose.

The differences in the value of the health insurance benefit the contractor is offering and what is currently available to TSOs who work for TSA are enormous. We can begin our comparison by noting that the contractor offers only one choice; FEHBP offers 11 choices in Nation-wide plans and an additional two specific to Montana. The contractor offers only a high-deductible plan with premiums of $54.39 a pay period for individual coverage and $190.63 for family coverage. The Nation-wide high-deductible FEHBP plan from GEHA costs TSOs $50.87 a pay period for individual coverage and $116.18 for family coverage—a 40% difference. But the differences in premiums are only the beginning. Because preventive services are only covered "in network" in Tennessee in the contractor's plan at 100% without the deductible, participants would have to pay 50% after the deductible for all preventive services—including children's and women's well care, annual mammograms, cervical cancer screenings, prostate cancer screenings, and immunizations. In contrast, the GEHA plan in FEHBP available to TSOs in Montana pays 100% in network (with network providers in Montana available) and 75% after the deductible out of network. Out-of-pocket maximum for the contractor are $5,500 and $11,000 for individual and family coverage in network in Tennessee—but in Montana, out of network, the out-of-pocket maximum each year is $11,000 for individuals and a whopping $22,000 for families. In contrast, the out-of-pocket maximum for the GEHA high-deductible plan is $5,000 for individuals and $10,000 for families.

Although there are many more differences, another important one is that the GEHA high-deductible plan under FEHBP allows for a Health Savings Account (HSA) or a Health Reimbursement Account (HRA) and the contractor's plan allows only a HRA. HRAs offer a vastly inferior economic benefit to the employee, because unlike HSAs, assets in an HRA do not earn interest and are forfeited by the employee if he switches health plans or leaves the job for reasons other than retirement. They belong to the employer, not the employee. An employer uses an HRA to pay for actual health care costs incurred by their employees. With an HSA, employer contributions are made whether or not the costs are incurred, and an employee gets to keep all unused HSA contributions made by both themselves and their employer when they leave the job. Indeed, because HRAs benefit only the employer, the "Arrangement" undermines the incentive systems on which high deductible plans are based. The employee has far less incentive to minimize expenditures, since the money belongs not to him, but rather to his boss.

This is not nearly an exhaustive description of the ways that the contractor's health care plan is of inferior value to the employee as compared to the high-deductible plan available to TSOs in Montana under FEHBP. But it suffices to show how the contractor's plan does not comport with the statutory requirement for a "qualified private screening company" under § 44920 of ATSA that benefits offered are "not less than the level of compensation and other benefits" provided to TSOs. Of course, the benefits in FEHBP's high-deductible plan are less generous than those in the other 10 plans made available to TSOs. If one interprets the statutory language to mean the range of value of the benefits, than the contractor's plan is of less value than the least valuable FEHBP plan. TSOs in Montana now have the choice of the GEHA plan, as well as the following additional Nation-wide plans:

    (1) Blue Cross Blue Shield Standard Option
    (2) Blue Cross Blue Shield Basic Option
    (3) NALC
    (4) GEHA Benefit Plan
    (5) Mailhandlers Benefit Value Plan
    (6) SAMBA
    (7) Mailhandlers Standard
    (8) APWU Health Plan
    (9) Mailhandlers Benefit Plan Consumer Option
    (10) NALC Value Option Plan

And two additional Montana plans:

    (1) Aetna Healthfund HDHP for South/Southeast/Western Montana
    (2) Aetna HealthFund CDHP and Value Plan, South/Southeast/Western Mt. areas.

While it is difficult to quantify the economic value of choice among 13 plans versus no choice, no one could describe an employer offering only one choice as providing a benefit that is "not less than the level" of benefit offered by the Federal Government.

Thus far, we conducted an apples-to-apples comparison of the contractor's health insurance plan and the Government's worst plan, even though the contractor's plan is clearly a rotten apple. But how about comparing it to the best plan FEHBP has to offer TSAs—and by "best" I mean most popular: Blue Cross Blue Shield's Standard option, the choice of over 60% of Federal employees.

COMPARISON OF CONTRACTOR HEALTH PLAN VS. FEHBP PLANS AVAILABLE TO TSOS AT TSA

Type of Coverage	Contractor Plan**	Contractor Plan**	GEHA High Deductible*	GEHA High Deductible*	BCBS Standard*	BCBS Standard*
	Biweekly Employee Premium	Biweekly Employer Premium	Biweekly Employee Premium	Biweekly Employer Premium	Biweekly Employee Premium	Biweekly Employer Premium
Self Only	$54.39	n/a	$50.87	$152.60	$87.82	$196.68
Self and Family	190.63	n/a	116.18	384.54	204.98	437.62

**CSSI Firstline Documents provided to AFGE.

*http://www.opm.gov/healthcare-insurance/healthcare/plan-information/premiums/2014/nonpostal-hmo.pdf.

As is clear from the above, the economic value of the health insurance benefit, as measured by the employer cost for provision of the benefit, shows clearly that the contractor's plan is inferior. We know that the actuarial value of the benefits of both the contractor's plan and the GEHA high-deductible plan are lower than the Blue Cross Blue Shield Standard Option Plan. But we have shown that the GEHA plan offers superior benefits, and although we do not know the contractor's cost for the HRA/High Deductible plan, we know that it is far lower than TSA's costs for either the GEHA or the BCBS plan, and thus does not meet the standard in the statute.

The contractor appears not to provide any retirement benefit at all. There is no mention of a pension plan: No 401(K) savings plan, no profit-sharing plan, no simplified employee pension plan (SEP) or IRA, no money purchase pension plan, no cash balance plan, no stock bonus plan, and no employee stock ownership plan. In short, this employer does not even make the smallest gesture toward the benefit equivalence that the statute demands in the area of retirement income security.

Incumbent Montana TSOs report TSA management has been slow to respond to their many questions about the transition to SPP and often receive contradictory information. In comparison, TSA has held TSOs to tight deadlines for life-altering decisions. Although the collective bargaining agreement negotiated between AFGE and TSA includes a provision that creates a permanent Voluntary Transfer Option, TSOs were only given 10 calendar days to review a vacancy list (that did not include all TSO job vacancies listed on USAJobs), pick five airports and complete an on-line application. TSA failed to hold itself to the same timely responses required of TSOs: TSOs report that their airport's Human Resources (HR) offices provided delayed and contradictory responses to questions. TSOs were told by HR offices that they would not qualify for unemployment compensation because they were entitled to "Priority Placement" with CSSI/Firstline. The so-called "right" of "Priority Placement" or "Right of First Refusal" is qualified and unenforceable, and decisions regarding unemployment compensation eligibility are made by the State of Montana, not TSA employees. Long-term TSOs report that they were repeatedly told they would not be eligible for severance pay if they separated from TSA, would be penalized for early retirement, and would not receive unemployment compensation.

CONGRESS SHOULD NOT LIMIT ITS SPP OVERSIGHT TO THE TREATMENT OF CONTRACTORS

In their January 14, 2014 testimony before the Government Operations Subcommittee of the Oversight and Government Reform Committee, GAO confirmed that TSA has failed to track the performance of contract screeners in the same manner that TSO performance is endlessly scrutinized. The SPP screener attrition rates, covert testing failures, TIP, and other performance measures are unknown to the public. Just as the news media recently reported that an intoxicated man impersonated a screener at the privatized San Francisco International Airport and groped several female passengers, the public was only made aware of covert test cheating and other security breaches at SPP airports when reported by journalists. AFGE believes that much of the negative public perception of TSOs by some members of the public is fueled by the agency's rush to report unproven allegations against TSOs while security contractors and their employees have never faced the same level of relentless scrutiny. The Contract Screener Reform and Accountability Act (H.R. 4115) provides the reform and transparency program badly needs. The bill's sponsors, Homeland Security Ranking Member Bennie Thompson, Committee Member Sheila Jackson Lee, and Appropriations Committee Ranking Member Nita Lowey, have a history of being champions of the TSO workforce, being fiercely committed to our Nation's aviation security, and have long sought transparency and accountability in the SPP. H.R. 4115 is a significant step in ensuring all of aviation security, not just that which is performed by Federal employees, receives the oversight necessary to protect the flying public.

H.R. 4115 would make these significant improvements to the SPP program:
- Bans the subsidiaries of foreign-owned corporations from obtaining SPP contracts.
- Requires covert testing of contract screeners and penalizes cheating on those tests;
- Protects TSO jobs and benefits if a security contractor is awarded a contract at their airport;
- Protects those who disclose wrongdoing by private screening companies;
- Requires reporting of security breaches by private screening companies; and
- Ensures transparency by requiring a cost analysis of private screening companies to be conducted by the Comptroller General.

The relevance of the Contract Screener Reform and Accountability Act to the SPP, the TSO workforce, and aviation security cannot be understated. H.R. 4115 should be passed by the House.

CONCLUSION

A video of the checkpoint at Washington-Dulles International Airport taken the morning of September 11, 2001 shows several hijackers being allowed to pass by several private screeners even though they set off metal detector alarms. We now know those men were allowed to board American Airlines Flight 77 with "utility knives" that they would use to kill innocent passengers and crew on-board the plane, and begin the hijacking of that flight. No individual private screener is responsible for the tragedy that occurred. However the country cannot turn a blind eye to the circumstances that led to the ultimate aviation security breach, including the issues raised by placing this important work in the hands of private security contractors. Screening of passengers and baggage remains inherently Governmental work that should remain with the Federal TSO workforce.

Mr. HUDSON. Thank you, Mr. Cox.

We appreciate all of you being here. I now recognize myself for 5 minutes to ask questions.

Let me start, Ms. Martin, by saying it should never have taken 5 years to be able to convert to private screeners and, frankly, it is an unacceptable amount of time.

Nonetheless, I appreciate your perseverance because, like you, I see benefits—substantial benefits of privatized screening and, like you, I welcome the kind of efficiencies and customer service improvements that the private sector brings to bear in the airport environment.

Having gone through the process yourself, what advice would you give other airports that are interested in the SPP program?

Ms. MARTIN. Barring any changes to the current process, I would tell them to be prepared for a—the long haul. That is the best I could tell them. Unfortunately, there just isn't—aren't any guidelines where you could tell them where they could find efficiencies.

If I may, if—I would tell them to outline a process with TSA on the front end and then identify milestones along the way and to have a point person that they can contact on a regular basis for information about the process.

Mr. HUDSON. I appreciate that.

Mr. VanLoh, would you like to respond to this question as well?

Mr. VANLOH. I would agree with Ms. Martin. It is a long haul. Fortunately, Kansas City was selected right out of the box. If we had to go through this process—this onerous process now with the changing environment in our city government, I am not so sure we would be successful.

Mr. HUDSON. That is troubling.

Mr. Amitay, in your testimony, you brought up that private companies can bring increased levels of efficiency and effectiveness to the security screening process.

Why is it that private screening companies are able to do screening cheaper with same or better results, in your opinion?

Mr. AMITAY. Well, I think, with private screening companies, they just have—they are able to create incentives and disincentives for the workers that result in better attendance and timeliness and in performance, all of which can save money.

A major cost-driver in any hourly operation is overtime cost and being able to schedule more efficiently, being able to staff more efficiently, having more robust attendance policies, you know, as Mark mentioned, greater discipline.

That can all cut down on the personnel costs, which are the major factor. But, also, with the—with the management administrative costs, the ability of private sector to save over the Federal sectors is astronomical.

You know, just take one issue such as leasing space at an airport. You know, TSA, I think at San Francisco, they have got some pretty prime space at the airport, whereas, the screening company—you know, they are very cost-efficient in their leasing. Private companies also greatly monitor workers' compensation claims and try to reduce injury rates. Again, that is another major cost-driver.

You know, TSA really doesn't have any incentive to lower workers' compensation claims and, as I mentioned before with absenteeism, that is a major problem at TSA. Those are huge cost drivers.

Mr. HUDSON. When you talk about costs, you know, one of the constant frustrations I hear is that TSA is not counting all the cost to the Federal Government, as you mentioned in your testimony, including these retirement costs.

I mean, why is it important for us to include all that when we are comparing the cost to the private sector?

Mr. AMITAY. Well, I think, as the FAA Modernization Act amendments to ATSA—they made a good point. They said that the private screener should not detrimentally affect cost efficiency as well as performance at an airport.

So, therefore, yes, the private screeners need to be as costly or less than Federal screeners. But—so, therefore, the Federal Government then will set a cost ceiling for the private screeners at an airport, and this is the bid ceiling.

If the—if TSA is not including all the costs of Federal screeners in that bid ceiling for private screening, well, then the private screeners will necessarily have to bid lower than what it costs the Federal Government.

Now, they are able to do that because of some of these cost efficiencies I've mentioned, but it is making the bids artificially lower than they need to be.

Mr. HUDSON. Makes sense.

Well, my time is about to expire. So I don't want to abuse my right. That limits my ability to gavel some of the others down when they go over.

So at this time I will conclude my questions for the first round and recognize the gentleman from Montana, Mr. Daines, for any questions he may have.

Mr. DAINES. Thanks, Mr. Chairman. I appreciate that.

Question for Ms. Martin: What is the overall level of interaction that you have had with TSA's SPP office?

Ms. MARTIN. I am sorry. If you could repeat that.

Mr. DAINES. What is the overall level of interaction you have had with TSA's SPP office?

Ms. MARTIN. The level?

Mr. DAINES. Uh-huh.

Ms. MARTIN. Little to none. You know, we—when we started this process, we spoke with the folks in the SPP office initially. We were told where to find the application on-line.

When we were first—took our application to the District of Columbia the first time, we met with the SPP office, who encouraged us to apply at that time so that they could lump it in with the seven airports in eastern Montana. We chose, along with the other airports in Montana, to hold our application.

After we brought our application and applied in 2009, there was little to no interaction between the office except that which we initiated, asking where things were in the process. That has been pretty much the case through the entire process.

Mr. DAINES. So I think your response to my—answers the next question, but I will ask it anyway.

Would you say you are generally satisfied or dissatisfied with the amount of information you received from TSA regarding the SPP process?

Ms. MARTIN. I would say I was dissatisfied.

Mr. DAINES. What improvements do you think could be made to SPP that would make the process of applying as well as transitioning to private screening easier for airports without sacrificing the necessary security?

Ms. MARTIN. You know, the application process itself is quite easy. I think there were a few questions on the application that would be more telling. As they say, when you have seen one airport, you have seen one airport. We all differ.

Being able to identify the unique, perhaps, seasonality or other things that happen at that airport, that would be important in staffing. I think also then identifying the process milestones so that an applicant knows exactly when things are going to happen and at what point.

It would be lovely to be involved in the—in, actually, the decision with regard to the final contractor to make certain that those things which were proposed in the scope of work actually do fit the needs of that airport.

If the process is going to continue to be a lengthy one—things actually could have changed at that airport in terms of seasonality or service, new carriers, what have you, that could actually have changed the demand from when the SOP was—the RFP was written and when it was actually awarded.

Mr. DAINES. So, from your viewpoint, going through this process—this nearly 5-year process, do you believe that airports are discouraged from applying and participating in SPP with the nature of the application and procurement process? Were you encouraged or discouraged to go through that process?

Ms. MARTIN. You know, a number of the airport managers that I have talked to that have heard our story say, "Boy, I wouldn't do that." So I believe that they are discouraged. I think, if more people heard our story, they would be discouraged.

Mr. DAINES. Could you describe the general sentiment in the airport community towards private screening, in general, if you could?

Ms. MARTIN. I am sorry. Say that first part again.

Mr. DAINES. Could you describe the general sentiment in the airport community towards private screening, in general?

Ms. MARTIN. You know, I don't know that I can speak for all of my counterparts at the other airports, but I think, by and large, we all believe that it can be done.

Being a Federal employee doesn't make you impervious or make you perfect that the same people are going to do the job as for the private screener.

I think we are concerned more about the management and the staffing, and we believe that the private screener can be flexible and can manage that.

Mr. DAINES. So I heard Mr. Cox's testimony as well just talking about the Bozeman airport. In fact, that is my home airport. I fly in and out of there every week. I live about 10 miles away from the airport.

What—what would you say in terms of kind-of the before and after as it relates to employee satisfaction, as it relates to the quality of the security now moving—transitioning to private screening? What is your sense of the kind-of before and after?

Ms. MARTIN. Well, since we haven't actually made the transition, although roughly about 40 percent of our workforce is going to be going over to the private screener, they seem to be excited and happy. We haven't noticed any change in the delivery of their job.

Those that are either deciding to leave the workforce completely or move to other airports cite various reasons. But I believe that the workforce that is staying is happy with the transition.

Mr. DAINES. Okay. Question for Mr. Amitay: What—I heard some pretty strong statements from Mr. Cox there as it relates to kind-of before and after there.

What has been your experience, No. 1? No. 2, in general, how many different private screening companies compete for these contracts typically?

Mr. AMITAY. In terms of the competition, I don't have the exact numbers. But I would say probably a half dozen offers are under the FCE for a typical SPP contract. There hasn't been that many of them.

You know, the Kansas City recompete and the Montana solicitation were some of the two most recent. I know, also, there is two in Florida. But it—there is a good deal of competition.

Mr. DAINES. Then maybe just contrasting maybe what your experience has been—I heard Mr. Cox talk about the experience in the Bozeman airport—what have you seen kind-of before and after, perhaps, in your experience?

Mr. AMITAY. Well, unfortunately, because of TSA's management of the program, there has been very few, actually, airports that have converted from Federal screeners to private screeners.

Kansas City and San Francisco, the two largest airports that use private screeners, were part of that original pilot program. So, really, Montana—meaning that they never switched from private—they never had Federal screeners.

So Montana is a little bit of a laboratory in terms of the transition. So people are watching that, and we are hopeful that, you know, it will be done effectively to benefit all the parties involved.

Mr. DAINES. Okay. Thank you.

Mr. HUDSON. Thank you.

The Chairman now recognizes the gentleman from South Carolina, Mr. Sanford, for any questions you may have.

Mr. SANFORD. Thank you, Mr. Chairman.

I will quickly yield my time to you, sir, or to my colleague from Montana, in the event he wants more time. I have been at conference and, therefore, did not get to hear your testimony.

I do have one just general question just on private screening at large. It is my understanding that, basically, the bulk of all Western countries use private screening. So, you know, are there some best practices out there that you have identified in other countries that are worth noting?

No. 2, you know, why is it—I remember at the time of 9/11 calling a couple of former colleagues up here and saying, "If this isn't a gut check, I don't know what is."

I see a former colleague from Tennessee back there, in fact.

You know, the idea of Federalizing 40,000 folks just seemed to me a big jump without a lot of experimentation leading up to it.

Why not more in the reverse, in terms of more experimentation from the standpoint of using private contractors in this particular regard?

I would love to hear a couple of your thoughts just at large on that front.

Then I will yield to you, Mr. Chairman.

Mr. AMITAY. Well, Congressman, I believe that the reason why people utilize private screening in other countries is because, first of all, the idea that the Government is both a regulator and the operator is very a dangerous proposition sometimes.

You know, as has been the case already with TSA, you know, not to bring up bad stories, but, in Hawaii, it goes something like 39 TSA people at the airport, including the Federal security director and screeners and another—were fired and another 17 were disciplined because of, really, a large-scale concerted operation to not follow the proper required screening procedures.

You know, when you have a—you know, when you have an arm's-length relationship with TSA doing—setting the policies and doing the regulation and then a private screening company doing the operations, you know, that private screening company is going to do what it is supposed to do because, also, it realizes that, you know, it could lose that contract, it could be debarred, or other punitive measures can be taken against it so it won't be able to do it anymore. This doesn't exist in the Federal screening world. So, you know, that—that is a major consideration, I think, that other countries have.

In terms of best practices, you know, private screening companies, they are constantly looking for best practices because they constantly have to improve because they face constant competition, you know, from other competitors. If they don't employ best practices in terms of scheduling and screening and in terms of screener oversight——

Mr. SANFORD. I understand.

But are there two that you would recommend to the committee worth noting or worth looking at either from the standpoint of the company or from the standpoint of a country?

Mr. AMITAY. I think everything is worth looking at, you know, again, with the basic premise that, you know, TSA sets—they set the security requirements. They set the standard operating procedures.

But if there are innovative and effective and efficient ways to meet those TSA security requirements, then they should be allowed to be explored.

Mr. SANFORD. I yield back, Mr. Chairman.

Mr. HUDSON. Thank you, Mr. Sanford.

One of the issues that Mr. Cox raised was concerning to me, just about the compensation equivalencies. You know, obviously, I have had the opportunity in this job to meet a lot of TSOs.

There are a lot of heroic, patriotic Americans working for TSA. You know, we certainly—you know, our concerns to find efficiencies and a better way of doing things through SPPs does not in any way reflect our opinion about these employees.

But I don't know if—Mr. Amitay, do you want to respond to what Mr. Cox was saying about the situation in Montana where this TSO is not apparently getting equivalent compensation and benefits?

Mr. AMITAY. Well, I think that there are some misconceptions about exactly the compensation being offered to the TSOs who are transitioning, you know.

I understand that those TSOs that are transitioning are going to get the same hourly wages and that, yeah, the benefits plan—it will be competitive. Will it be the exact benefits plan the Federal Government offers? No.

But nobody in the private sector offers the exact benefits plan the Federal Government does. It is just out-of-date.

Mr. HUDSON. What about the concern about the health care plan only being available in Tennessee?

Mr. AMITAY. That is absolutely untrue. I—you know, whatever evidence or proof you need that it is untrue I can provide. I mean, that absolutely makes no sense.

You know, this is a Blue Cross Blue Shield plan and, through Blue Cross Blue Shield—even though it might be administered out of Tennessee or based through the Tennessee plan, they have these reciprocity agreements through these Blue Cross Blue Shield State associations.

So, therefore, you know, those Montana Blue Cross Blue Shield, you know, providers, you know, are considered to be in-house providers under a Tennessee Blue Cross Blue Shield plan.

Mr. HUDSON. All right. Well, I appreciate that.

Mr. VanLoh, you talked about the contract award process you are involved in now and is back in litigation and the concerns that, because the standard is sort-of the minimum pay scale, you have got a lot of employees who have been there maybe even 12 years now with the current contractor, and you expressed some of the concerns you have with what that impact will have on the workforce.

Do you want to elaborate on that a little bit?

Mr. VANLOH. Thank you, Mr. Chairman.

Well, that is absolutely true. When you have got a screening supervision staff that may have been there for the entire 12 years since 9/11, those senior—that senior capability will be gone because the company that was the apparent low bidder even low-bid the TSA's own estimate by far, by several million dollars.

So, naturally, with a labor-intensive contract, the way you are going to save is cutting salaries and hours of work. So we—we see a mass migration of our senior-experience screeners to other employment because of the cuts just to make the contract work.

Mr. HUDSON. Well, in the initial SPP contract, you were able to give input in terms of vendor, is my understanding. Was that not part of the process when you—when you are renewing this or re-bidding this?

Mr. VANLOH. I have been involved with two renewal contracts since I have been in Kansas City 11 years. Usually, a 1- to 2-day session where all the bidders come into town, we are not part of that. We have no idea of who is actually bidding on the contract. We are not asked about our incumbent on how they are doing.

We get the letters from the public. TSA usually doesn't get complaint letters. We do. So we know how we are performing. We are not asked. Then we read about it on-line or in the papers on who the low bidder is and the new contract award. That is how the airport finds out.

Mr. HUDSON. That doesn't seem to make sense to me, especially, when you do a new SPP bid, the airport is allowed to comment on it. I don't know why there wouldn't be input allowed later when it actually would be more-informed comments, in my opinion. So I appreciate that.

Mr. Sanford, are you interested in a second round?

Mr. SANFORD. I defer to you right now.

Mr. HUDSON. Okay. Well, in that case, I want to thank the witnesses for your time and your testimony. I think this was very informative. I appreciate you being here with us today.

At this time I will dismiss the first panel and call up the second panel. Thank you.

I will now call the second panel. First, we have Mr. William Benner, who currently serves as the director of the Screening Partnership Program. He joined TSA in 2002 and has served in numerous positions. Prior to joining TSA, Mr. Benner spent 21 years as an army military police officer and public affairs officer. In his final military assignment, Mr. Benner served as a DOD liaison to the newly-created FBI counterterrorism division, where he cultivated collaborative relationships between DOD, FBI, and other Federal agencies.

Ms. Jennifer Grover is an acting director of GAO's Homeland Security and Justice Team, leading a portfolio of work on transportation security issues. Prior to this position, Ms. Grover was an assistant director of GAO's health care team, where she led reviews on a diverse range of health care-related issues. Ms. Grover joined GAO in 1991.

The witnesses' full statements will appear in the record. Thank you both for joining us. The Chairman now recognize Mr. Benner to testify.

STATEMENT OF WILLIAM BENNER, SCREENING PARTNERSHIP PROGRAM, OFFICE OF SECURITY OPERATIONS, TRANSPORTATION SECURITY ADMINISTRATION, U.S. DEPARTMENT OF HOMELAND SECURITY

Mr. BENNER. Chairman Hudson, Ranking Member Richmond, and Members of the subcommittee. I am pleased to appear before you today to discuss the TSA Screening Partnership Program. The SPP is a voluntary program under which airports may apply to utilize private-sector, rather than TSA employees to conduct passenger screening.

Upon an airport's acceptance into the program, TSA selects a company that meets statutory requirements to conduct screening services under contract with the Federal Government.

Regardless of whether an airport has private or Federal employees conducting passenger screening operations, TSA maintains responsibility for transportation security.

SPP participation depends on interest from airport operators. Eighteen airports are currently participating in SPP and either have private contract screeners in place or are in the process of transitioning to contract screeners.

These 18 airports represent approximately 4.5 percent of TSA's annual passenger volume. Airport operators interested in participating in the SPP may find the application on the TSA website, along with an overview of the application process and additional relevant information.

TSA also utilizes the Federal Business Opportunities website to communicate with a wide range of vendors on SPP-related topics. For example, TSA advertised and held an SPP-specific industry day in January 2014, which was attended by approximately 100 vendors. The industry day provided an overview of the program's direction and goals, informed industry of the acquisition process, and offered a forum for obtaining feedback and insight into industry capabilities.

TSA has also met with vendors in other forums, such as the National Association of Security Companies' annual Washington Summit and the Washington Homeland Security Roundtable, both held in June 2014.

The FAA Modernization and Reform Act of 2012 provided standards for approval of an SPP application, a time line for approving or denying applications, and specific actions to take in the event an application is denied. Additionally, under the act, the TSA administrator must determine that the approval would not compromise the security or detrimentally effect the cost efficiency or effectiveness of the screening of passengers or property at the airport.

In order to maintain cost efficiency, as required by the FAA authorization, TSA includes the Federal cost estimate of the airport screening operations in all requests for proposals. This practice demonstrates compliance with the law by ensuring that all offerors are evaluated on proposed costs as well as their ability to perform airport screening according to TSA standards.

The methodology used to develop Federal cost estimates is continually validated and refined to conform with changes to the law, as well as to incorporate improvements resulting from audits conducted by the GAO and the DHS Office of Inspector General.

TSA's goal is to award a contract within 1 year of receiving a new SPP application, assuming all legal requirements are met, and a qualified contractor is identified during the procurement process.

While this is an aggressive time line, given the Federal Acquisition Regulation requirements, the goal is a reflection of our commitment to ensure airports that choose to have contract screeners can move expeditiously in that direction.

The first opportunity to meet that 1-year goal is with the application we recently received from the Portsmouth International Airport in June 2014. It is my responsibility as the senior executive in charge of SPP to ensure the program is managed with an appropriate focus on both cost and security. I appreciate the work that the GAO and this committee have done in partnering with us to achieve the goal.

Thank you for the opportunity to appear here today. I'll be happy to answer your questions.

[The prepared statement of Mr. Benner follows:]

PREPARED STATEMENT OF WILLIAM BENNER

JULY 29, 2014

Chairman Hudson, Ranking Member Richmond, and Members of the subcommittee, I am pleased to appear before you today to discuss the Transportation Security Administration (TSA) Screening Partnership Program (SPP).

As you know, TSA is a high-performing counterterrorism agency charged with facilitating and securing the travel of the nearly 1.8 million air passengers each day. Our workforce carries out the important mission of protecting the transportation system to ensure freedom of movement for people and commerce. TSA's security measures comprise a multi-layered system that identifies, manages, and mitigates risk. Combined, these layers form a strong, secure system designed to deter and prevent terrorist attacks.

SCREENING PARTNERSHIP PROGRAM (SPP) HISTORY

Congress, through the Aviation and Transportation Security Act (ATSA) (Pub. L. 107–71), established TSA and determined that passenger screening should be a predominantly Federal responsibility. ATSA also authorized a pilot program for privatized passenger screening (see 49 U.S.C. § 44919). TSA selected five airports to participate in the pilot program, representing five airport security risk categories as defined by the TSA administrator. Companies that met statutory qualifications were then selected to conduct screening services under contract with the Federal Government. Further, these private-sector employees are required to maintain the qualification criteria of Federal Transportation Security Officers (TSOs), and to receive compensation no less than such Federal personnel. This provision was formalized into the Screening Partnership Program after the 2-year pilot period concluded.

The Federal Aviation Administration (FAA) Modernization and Reform Act of 2012 (Pub. L. 112–95) amended 49 U.S.C. § 44920 to provide standards for approval of an SPP application, a time line for approving or denying applications, and specific actions to take in the event an application is denied. Additionally, the TSA administrator must determine "that the approval would not compromise the security or detrimentally affect the cost-efficiency or the effectiveness of the screening of passengers or property at the airport."

The SPP is a voluntary program whereby airports may apply for SPP status and employ private security companies to conduct airport screening according to TSA standards. Participation depends on interest from airport operators. Since the program began in 2004, 31 airports have applied, including the original statutory 5 pilot airports. Of those 31, 18 are currently participating in the SPP program, and either have private contract screeners in place or are in the process of transitioning to contract screeners. Of these 18 airports, 8 fall within the smallest airport classification (Category IV—which means they enplane between 2,500 and 10,000 passengers a year). The 18 airports currently participating in SPP represent approximately 28.9 million passengers per year, or 4.5% of TSA's annual passenger volume.

The cumulative contract value for these 18 airports is currently $661 million over a 5-year period.

Of the remaining 13 airports that have applied to the program, one is currently in the application adjudication phase, two are in the source selection phase, and the remaining 10 have either discontinued commercial air service, have been denied, or have withdrawn their applications prior to contract award.

Regardless of whether an airport has private or Federal employees conducting passenger screening operations, TSA maintains overall responsibility for transportation security. As new and emerging threats are identified, we must be able to adapt and modify our procedures quickly to protect the traveling public. Federal Security Directors oversee the contracted security screening operations to ensure compliance with Federal security standards throughout the aviation network.

TRANSPARENCY AND INDUSTRY ENGAGEMENT

Airport operators interested in participating in the SPP, may find the application on the TSA website along with an, an overview of the application process, and additional information relevant to airport operators contemplating participation. Additionally, the TSA website provides a listing and map of SPP airports, recent news regarding SPP (such as contract awards), links to Requests for Proposals (RFPs) postings, and employment opportunities at SPP service providers. TSA also utilizes the Federal Business Opportunities website to communicate with a wide range of vendors on SPP-related topics. For example, TSA advertised and held an SPP-specific Industry Day on January 10, 2014. This meeting was attended by approximately 100 vendors and provided a general overview of the program's direction and goals, informed industry of the acquisition process, and also offered a forum for obtaining feedback and insight into industry capabilities. TSA has also met with vendors in other forums, such as the National Association of Security Companies Annual Washington Summit and the Washington Homeland Security Roundtable, both held in June 2014.

COST EFFICIENCY

In order to maintain cost efficiency as required by the FAA authorization, restrain costs from exceeding those incurred by TSA for Federal screening, and creating an unfunded requirement, the agency includes the Federal cost estimate of the airport screening operation in the RFP. This new practice demonstrates compliance with the law by ensuring that bidders are evaluated on costs as well as their ability to conduct airport screening according to TSA standards. Estimates are developed in accordance with standard methodology using the most recent and actual data from the airport. The methodology is continually validated and refined to conform with changes to the law, as well as to incorporate improvements resulting from audits conducted by the Government Accountability Office (GAO) and the Department of Homeland Security Office of the Inspector General (OIG).

PROGRAM ACCOMPLISHMENTS

In his January 2014 testimony, TSA's assistant administrator for the Office of Security Operations, Kelly Hoggan, stated that TSA's goal is to award a contract within 1 year of receiving a new SPP application, assuming all legal requirements are met and a qualified contractor is identified during the procurement process. While this is an aggressive time line given the requirements of the Federal Acquisition Regulation, the goal is a reflection of our commitment to ensure airports that choose to have contract screeners can move expeditiously in that direction. The first opportunity to meet that 1-year goal is with the application we recently received from Portsmouth International Airport in June 2014.

Our programmatic efforts in recent months have been focused on completing the procurement process for airport applications that have already been approved. I am pleased to report that TSA awarded a contract for four Montana airports, also known as Montana West, which became effective on June 1, 2014. We are currently in the transition phase for converting the screening operations at these airports from Federal to contractor. Two more airports are nearing the end of the procurement process: Orlando Sanford International Airport and Sarasota Bradenton International Airport. TSA expects to award those contracts in the coming months, assuming we identify a qualified vendor from the procurement process.

TSA also closed out its remaining OIG recommendation to streamline the SPP application review process. In closing the recommendation, we instituted improvements in our processes for application review that will facilitate meeting the aggressive 1-year goal to award a contract on new applications. Process improvements include reducing the number of offices required to review and provide data for application decisions to only those essential to meet legislative requirements (security and cost efficiency) and co-locating the program and acquisitions teams that participate in the application review and procurement functions to enhance collaboration in planning and execution.

I would also like to mention that the Joint Statement of Managers accompanying the fiscal year 2014 Appropriations directed TSA to allocate resources for an independent study of the performance of Federalized compared to privatized airports in a number of areas, to include cost and security effectiveness. TSA awarded a contract in June 2014 to begin that study. We expect the contractor to publish the first of two reports in November 2014. The first report directly answers the Joint Statement of Managers and will be provided to GAO for review and subsequent reporting to Congress. The second report, focused on reviewing TSA's methodology for comparing performance and costs, will be completed in March 2015.

CONCLUSION

TSA strives to maximize security by keeping ahead of current threats identified by intelligence and by maintaining security systems that focus its resources on areas where they will yield the greatest benefit. This is consistent with our risk-based approach to security and critical in times of budget austerity. It is my responsibility as the senior executive in charge of SPP to ensure that the program is managed with an appropriate focus on cost and security. I appreciate the work that the Government Accountability Office and this committee have done in partnering with us to achieve this goal.

Thank you for the opportunity to appear here today. I will be happy to answer your questions.

Mr. HUDSON. Thank you, Mr. Benner.

The Chairman recognizes Ms. Grover to testify.

STATEMENT OF JENNIFER A. GROVER, ACTING DIRECTOR, HOMELAND SECURITY AND JUSTICE, GOVERNMENT ACCOUNTABILITY OFFICE

Ms. GROVER. Good morning Chairman Hudson, other Members, and staff. I am pleased to be here today to discuss TSA's implementation and oversight of the Screening Partnership Program.

My remarks today reflect the findings from GAO's previous studies of SPP. We have recently started a new study to examine TSA's current approach to comparing the cost of providing screening services at SPP and non-SPP airports.

At the end of 2012, GAO found weaknesses, both in TSA's implementation and in its oversight of SPP. First, regarding implementation, we found that TSA was not providing airports with clear guidance on how to apply to SPP. This is important to ensure that all airports have a full and fair opportunity to participate.

TSA offered on-line frequently asked questions, but little else. Airports told us that they needed help with several issues, such as understanding whether or not they were good candidates, how to complete the application, and what type of information that they were required to submit about costs.

Industry representatives echoed those concerns, noting that airports didn't want to invest in the application process when they were unsure about how they would be evaluated. But since then, consistent with our recommendation, TSA has posted additional guidance on its website, including examples of helpful information submitted by previous applicants, details about how applications will be assessed, and clarification about the requirements for submitting cost information.

Second, regarding oversight, in 2012, we found that TSA did not evaluate the relative performance of private and Federal screeners.

49

This is important because private screeners must be providing a level of services and protection that is equal or greater to that provided by the Federal screeners.

Therefore, we recommended that TSA regularly monitor screener performance at the SPP airports compared to non-SPP airports. At the time, they did have some performance measurements in place. They used a scorecard performance system to regularly assess screeners at every airport on numerous performance measures, but the result from that was a point-in-time snapshot of performance at that airport relative to its goals and relative to National averages, but not a comparison to the other airports in this category.

So, to address the question of comparative performance, GAO reviewed several years of performance data for the then 16 SPP airports on four different measures. We found that the private screeners did slightly better than Federal screeners on some measures and slightly worse on others.

Since then, TSA has started issuing its SPP annual reports, which, consistent with our recommendation, include performance data for each SPP airport relative to other airports in its category.

We are pleased that TSA's changes address our recommendations. These changes may assist TSA in making future improvements to the program. For example, with greater clarity and transparency in the application process, additional airports may be encouraged to apply. It may also help ensure that the application process is carried out in a consistent manner. With the new comparative performance data, TSA may be better-equipped to identify best practices, as well as to identify SPP airports that require additional attention to improve their performance.

Finally, one issue that remains unresolved is the question of the relative cost of screening operations at SPP versus non-SPP airports. Over the years, TSA has faced challenges in accurately comparing these costs. In previous work, we noted limitations in TSA's analysis, such as the need to analyze how changes in their underlying assumptions would affect cost estimates.

Since then, TSA has reported additional modifications to its cost estimation methodology. In our newly-initiated study, we will monitor TSA's progress in this area, and provide the committee with updated information.

Thank you for the opportunity to testify this morning. I look forward to your questions.

[The prepared statement of Ms. Grover follows:]

PREPARED STATEMENT OF JENNIFER A. GROVER

GAO HIGHLIGHTS

Highlights of GAO–14–787T, a testimony before the Subcommittee on Transportation Security, Committee on Homeland Security, House of Representatives.

Why GAO Did This Study

TSA maintains a Federal workforce to screen passengers and baggage at the majority of the Nation's commercial airports, but it also oversees a workforce of private screeners at airports who participate in the SPP. The SPP allows commercial airports to apply to have screening performed by private screeners, who are to provide a level of screening services and protection that equals or exceeds that of Federal screeners.

This testimony addresses the extent to which TSA: (1) Provides guidance to airport operators for the SPP application process, (2) assesses and monitors the performance of private versus Federal screeners, and (3) compares the costs of Federal and private screeners. This statement is based on reports and a testimony GAO issued from January 2009 through January 2014.

What GAO Recommends

GAO has made several recommendations since 2009 to improve SPP operations and oversight, which GAO has since closed as implemented based on TSA actions to address them.

SCREENING PARTNERSHIP PROGRAM.—TSA HAS IMPROVED APPLICATION GUIDANCE AND MONITORING OF SCREENER PERFORMANCE, AND CONTINUES TO IMPROVE COST COMPARISON METHODS

What GAO Found

Since GAO's December 2012 report on the Screening Partnership Program (SPP), the Transportation Security Administration (TSA) has developed guidance for airport operators applying to the SPP. In December 2012, GAO found that TSA had not provided guidance to airport operators on its SPP application and approval process, which had been revised to reflect statutory requirements. Further, airport operators GAO interviewed at the time identified difficulties in completing the revised application, such as obtaining cost information requested in the application. GAO recommended that TSA develop application guidance and TSA concurred. In December 2012, TSA updated its SPP website with general application guidance and a description of TSA's assessment criteria and process. The new guidance addresses the intent of GAO's recommendation.

TSA has also developed a mechanism to regularly monitor private versus Federal screener performance. In December 2012, TSA officials stated that they planned to assess overall screener performance across all commercial airports instead of comparing the performance of SPP and non-SPP airports as they had done previously. Also in December 2012, GAO reported differences between the performance at SPP and non-SPP airports based on screener performance data. In addition, GAO reported that TSA's across-the-board mechanisms did not summarize information for the SPP as a whole or across years, making it difficult to identify changes in private screener performance. GAO concluded that monitoring and comparing private and Federal screener performance were consistent with the statutory provision authorizing TSA to contract with private screening companies. As a result, GAO recommended that TSA develop a mechanism to regularly do so. TSA concurred with the recommendation and in January 2013, issued its SPP Annual Report, which provided an analysis of private versus Federal screener performance. In September 2013, TSA provided internal guidance requiring that the report annually verify that the level of screening services and protection provided at SPP airports is equal to or greater than the level that would be provided by Federal screeners. These actions address the intent of GAO's recommendation.

TSA has faced challenges in accurately comparing the costs of screening services at SPP and non-SPP airports. In 2007, TSA estimated that SPP airports cost about 17 percent more to operate than airports using Federal screeners. In January 2009, GAO noted strengths in TSA's methodology, but also identified seven limitations that could affect the accuracy and reliability of cost comparisons. GAO recommended that TSA update its analysis to address the limitations. TSA generally concurred with the recommendation. In March 2011, TSA described efforts to address the limitations and a revised cost comparison estimating that SPP airports would cost 3 percent more to operate in 2011 than airports using Federal screeners. In March 2011, GAO found that TSA had taken steps to address some of the limitations, but needed to take additional actions. In July 2014, TSA officials stated that they are continuing to make additional changes to the cost estimation methodology and GAO is continuing to monitor TSA's progress in this area through on-going work.

Chairman Hudson, Ranking Member Richmond, and Members of the subcommittee: I appreciate the opportunity to discuss our work on the Transportation Security Administration's (TSA) Screening Partnership Program (SPP). TSA, a component of the Department of Homeland Security (DHS), is responsible for ensuring the security of the traveling public through, among other things, screening passengers traveling by aircraft for explosives and other prohibited items. To fulfill this responsibility, TSA maintains a Federal workforce of screeners at a majority of the Nation's commercial airports, but also oversees a smaller workforce of private screeners employed by companies under contract to TSA at airports that participate in TSA's SPP.[1] The SPP, established in 2004 in accordance with provisions of the Aviation Transportation Security Act (ATSA), allows commercial airports an opportunity to "opt out" of Federal screening by applying to TSA to have private screeners perform the screening function.[2] At airports with private screeners, the screening of passengers and baggage is performed by private screening contractors selected and approved by TSA; however, TSA continues to be responsible for overseeing airport security operations and ensuring that the private contractors provide effective and efficient screening operations in a manner consistent with law and other TSA requirements at these airports.[3] As of July 2014, there are currently 18 airports participating in the program, 14 of which are currently operating with contracted screeners and four of which that have not yet transitioned to private screeners. Two additional approved airports are awaiting the selection of a screening contractor and one application is pending.[4]

The standard by which TSA evaluates airport applications for participation in the SPP has changed since the program's inception in 2004. First, in January 2011, the TSA administrator announced his decision not to expand the SPP beyond the 16 airports that were participating in the program at that time "unless a clear and substantial advantage to do so emerges in the future." In so doing, the administrator cited his interest in helping the agency evolve into a "more agile, high-performing organization that can meet the security threats of today and the future" as the reason for his decision. Of the 6 airports that submitted applications from March 2009 through January 2012 and that were evaluated under the "clear and substantial advantage" standard, TSA approved the application of 1 airport and denied the applications of the other 5. Second, according to TSA officials, the Federal Aviation Administration Modernization and Reform Act of 2012 (FAA Modernization Act), enacted in February 2012, prompted TSA to change the standard by which it evaluates SPP applications and requires, among other things, that the TSA administrator approve an SPP application submitted by an airport operator if the administrator determines that the approval would not compromise security or detrimentally affect the cost-efficiency or the effectiveness of the screening of passengers or property at the airport.[5]

My testimony today addresses the extent to which TSA: (1) Provides guidance to airport operators for the SPP application process, (2) assesses and monitors the performance of private versus Federal screeners, and (3) compares the costs of private and Federal operations. This statement is based on reports and a testimony we issued from January 2009 to January 2014.[6] Our March 2011 report was based on our review of TSA's updated cost analysis, which was provided in response to recommendations in our January 2009 report, as well as discussions with agency officials. For our December 2012 report, among other things we analyzed past and cur-

---

[1] For purposes of this report, a commercial airport is any airport in the United States that operates pursuant to a TSA-approved security program in accordance with 49 C.F.R. Pt. 1542 and at which TSA performs or oversees the performance of screening services. There are approximately 450 commercial airports as of July 2014. We refer to airports that are participating in the SPP as SPP airports and the screeners in those airports as private screeners. We refer to airports not participating in the SPP as non-SPP airports and the screeners in those airports as Federal screeners.

[2] See Pub. L. No. 107–71, §108, 115 Stat. 597, 611–13 (2001) (codified as amended at 49 U.S.C. §§44919–20). TSA established the SPP in 2004 after concluding a 2-year pilot program through which four private screening companies performed screening operations at 5 commercial airports (one contractor served 2 airports).

[3] The SPP contractor's responsibilities include recruiting, assessing, and training screening personnel to provide security screening functions in accordance with TSA regulations, policies, and procedures. SPP contractors are also expected to take operational direction from TSA to help ensure they meet the terms and conditions of the contract.

[4] In May 2014, TSA awarded contracts to 4 airports: Bert Mooney Airport, Bozeman Yellowstone International Airport, Glacier Park International Airport, and West Yellowstone Airport and in June 2014, TSA received a new application for Portsmouth International Airport. According to TSA, this application is in the adjudication phase with the decision to be made no later than October 2014.

[5] See Pub. L. No. 112–95, §830(a), 126 Stat. 11, 135 (2012) (codified at 49 U.S.C. §44920(b)). The term airport operator means a person that operates a "commercial airport," as that term is used in this report. See also 49 C.F.R. §1540.5 (defining the term "airport operator").

[6] GAO, *Aviation Security: TSA's Cost and Performance Study of Private-Sector Airport Screening*, GAO–09–27R (Washington, DC: Jan. 9, 2009); *Aviation Security: TSA's Revised Cost Comparison Provides a More Reasonable Basis for Comparing the Costs of Private-Sector and TSA Screeners* GAO–11–375R (Washington, DC Mar. 4, 2011); *Screening Partnership Program: TSA Should Issue More Guidance to Airports and Monitor Private Versus Federal Screener Performance*, GAO–13–208 (Washington, DC: Dec. 6, 2012); and *Screening Partnership Program: TSA Issued Application Guidance and Developed a Mechanism to Monitor Private Versus Federal Screener Performance*, GAO–14–269T (Washington, DC: Jan. 14, 2014).

rent SPP application forms and instructions and interviewed airport operators, screeners, SPP contractors, SPP applicants, TSA headquarters officials, and Federal security directors (FSD).[7] More detailed information on the scope and methodology appears in our January 2009, March 2011, and December 2012 reports, and our January testimony. For the January 2014 testimony, we obtained related documentation, such as the SPP Annual Report issued in January 2013, and interviewed agency officials on progress made to implement the recommendations from our December 2012 report related to application guidance and monitoring of private versus Federal screener performance.

We conducted the work on which this statement and the underlying products are based in accordance with generally accepted Government auditing standards. Those standards require that we plan and perform the audit to obtain sufficient, appropriate evidence to provide a reasonable basis for our findings and conclusions based on our audit objectives. We believe that the evidence obtained provides a reasonable basis for our findings and conclusions based on our audit objectives.

BACKGROUND

On November 19, 2002, pursuant to ATSA, TSA began a 2-year pilot program at 5 airports using private screening companies to screen passengers and checked baggage.[8] In 2004, at the completion of the pilot program, and in accordance with ATSA, TSA established the SPP, whereby any airport authority, whether involved in the pilot or not, could request a transition from Federal screeners to private, contracted screeners. All of the 5 pilot airports that applied were approved to continue as part of the SPP, and since its establishment, 21 additional airport applications have been accepted by the SPP.[9]

In March 2012, TSA revised the SPP application to reflect requirements of the FAA Modernization Act, enacted in February 2012.[10] Among other provisions, the act provides the following:

- Not later than 120 days after the date of receipt of an SPP application submitted by an airport operator, the TSA administrator must approve or deny the application.
- The TSA administrator shall approve an application if approval would not: (1) Compromise security, (2) detrimentally affect the cost efficiency of the screening of passengers or property at the airport, or (3) detrimentally affect the effectiveness of the screening of passengers or property at the airport.
- Within 60 days of a denial, TSA must provide the airport operator, as well as the Committee on Commerce, Science, and Transportation of the Senate and the Committee on Homeland Security of the House of Representatives, a written report that sets forth the findings that served as the basis of the denial, the results of any cost or security analysis conducted in considering the application, and recommendations on how the airport operator can address the reasons for denial.

All commercial airports are eligible to apply to the SPP. To apply, an airport operator must complete the SPP application and submit it to the SPP Program Management Office (PMO), as well as to the FSD for its airport. Figure 1 illustrates the SPP application process.

---

[7] FSDs are TSA officials that provide day-to-day operational direction for security operations at the airports within their jurisdiction, including those participating in the SPP.

[8] See 49 U.S.C. § 44919. The pilot program was to assess the feasibility of having qualified private screening companies provide airport security screening services in lieu of Federal screeners. The following airports from each security risk category were selected to participate: (1) San Francisco International Airport—Category X, (2) Kansas City International Airport—Category I, (3) Greater Rochester International Airport—Category II (now a Category I airport), (4) Jackson Hole Airport—Category III, and (5) Tupelo Regional Airport—Category IV. TSA classifies commercial airports in the United States into one of five security risk categories (X, I, II, III, and IV) based on various factors, such as the total number of takeoffs and landings annually, and other special security considerations. In general, Category X airports have the largest number of passenger boardings, and Category IV airports have the smallest.

[9] A total of 26 airports have been approved to participate in the SPP since its inception in 2004, including the 18 airports currently participating in the SPP (of which 4 airports have not yet transitioned to private screening), and 2 airports approved for participation and awaiting the selection of a screening contractor as of July 2014. Of the remaining 6 approved airports, 4 airports had participated in the SPP but left the program after commercial air service was discontinued at the airport and 2 withdrew their applications after being approved. For more information on the history of application to the SPP, see GAO–13–208.

[10] See generally Pub. L. No. 112–95, § 803, 126 Stat. at 135–36.

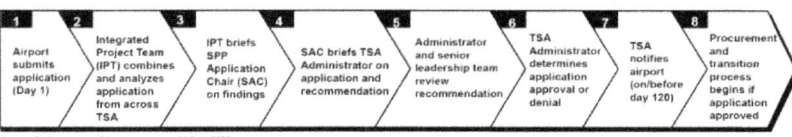

Figure 1: Transportation Security Administration's (TSA) Screening Partnership Program (SPP) Application Process

Source: GAO analysis of TSA information. | GAO-14-787T

Note: The IPT is made up of TSA staff from various offices across TSA, including offices related to human capital, information technology, security capabilities, and acquisitions.

Although TSA provides all airports with the opportunity to apply for participation in the SPP, authority to approve or deny the application resides in the discretion of the TSA administrator. According to TSA officials, in addition to the cost-efficiency and effectiveness considerations mandated by FAA Modernization Act, there are many other factors that are weighed in considering an airport's application for SPP participation. For example, the potential impacts of any upcoming projects at the airport are considered. Once an airport is approved for SPP participation and a private screening contractor has been selected by TSA, the contract screening workforce assumes responsibility for screening passengers and their property and is required to adhere to the same security regulations, standard operating procedures, and other TSA security requirements followed by Federal screeners at non-SPP airports.

TSA HAS DEVELOPED PROGRAM APPLICATION GUIDANCE TO HELP IMPROVE TRANSPARENCY OF ITS PROCESS AND ASSIST AIRPORTS IN COMPLETING THEIR APPLICATIONS

TSA has developed guidance to assist airport operators in completing their SPP applications, as we recommended in December 2012. Specifically, in December 2012, we reported that TSA had developed some resources to assist SPP applicants, but it had not provided guidance on its application and approval process to assist airports. As it was originally implemented in 2004, the SPP application process required only that an interested airport operator submit an application stating its intention to opt out of Federal screening as well as its reasons for wanting to do so. In 2011, TSA revised its SPP application to reflect the "clear and substantial advantage" standard announced by the administrator in January 2011. Specifically, TSA requested that the applicant explain how private screening at the airport would provide a clear and substantial advantage to TSA's security operations.[11] At that time, TSA did not provide written guidance to airports to assist them in understanding what would constitute a "clear and substantial advantage to TSA security operations" or TSA's basis for determining whether an airport had met that standard.

As previously noted, in March 2012 TSA again revised the SPP application in accordance with provisions of the FAA Modernization Act, which became law in February 2012. Among other things, the revised application no longer included the "clear and substantial advantage" question, but instead included questions that requested applicants to discuss how participating in the SPP would not compromise security at the airport and to identify potential areas where cost savings or efficiencies may be realized. In December 2012, we reported that while TSA provided general instructions for filling out the SPP application as well as responses to frequently asked questions (FAQ), the agency had not issued guidance to assist airports with completing the revised application or explained to airports how it would evaluate applications given the changes brought about by the FAA Modernization Act. For example, neither the application instructions nor the FAQs addressed TSA's SPP application evaluation process or its basis for determining whether an airport's entry into the SPP would compromise security or affect cost efficiency and effectiveness.

Further, in December 2012, we found that airport operators who completed the applications generally stated that they faced difficulties in doing so and that additional guidance would have been helpful.[12] For example, one operator stated that

---

[11] For more on the specific wording of this and other questions from the application, see GAO-13-208.

[12] For our December 2012 report, we interviewed four of the five airport operators that applied to the SPP since TSA revised its application after enactment of the FAA Modernization Act. All five of the applications were subsequently approved by TSA. We reported that three of the four operators we interviewed struggled to answer the application questions related to the cost-effi

Continued

he needed cost information to help demonstrate that his airport's participation in the SPP would not detrimentally affect the cost-efficiency of the screening of passengers or property at the airport and that he believed not presenting this information would be detrimental to his airport's application. However, TSA officials at the time said that airports do not need to provide this information to TSA because, as part of the application evaluation process, TSA conducts a detailed cost analysis using historical cost data from SPP and non-SPP airports. The absence of cost and other information in an individual airport's application, TSA officials noted, would not materially affect the TSA administrator's decision on an SPP application.

Therefore, we reported in December 2012 that while TSA had approved all applications submitted since enactment of the FAA Modernization Act, it was hard to determine how many more airports, if any, would have applied to the program had TSA provided application guidance and information to improve transparency of the SPP application process. Specifically, we reported that in the absence of such application guidance and information, it may be difficult for airport officials to evaluate whether their airports are good candidates for the SPP or determine what criteria TSA uses to accept and approve airports' SPP applications. We concluded that clear guidance for applying to the SPP could improve the transparency of the application process and help ensure that the existing application process is implemented in a consistent and uniform manner. Thus, we recommended that TSA develop guidance that clearly: (1) States the criteria and process that TSA is using to assess whether participation in the SPP would compromise security or detrimentally affect the cost efficiency or the effectiveness of the screening of passengers or property at the airport, (2) states how TSA will obtain and analyze cost information regarding screening cost efficiency and effectiveness and the implications of not responding to the related application questions, and (3) provides specific examples of additional information airports should consider providing to TSA to help assess an airport's suitability for the SPP.

TSA concurred with our recommendation and, in January 2014, we reported that TSA had taken actions to address it. Specifically, TSA updated its SPP website in December 2012 by providing: (1) General guidance to assist airports with completing the SPP application and (2) a description of the criteria and process the agency will use to assess airports' applications to participate in the SPP. While the guidance states that TSA has no specific expectations of the information an airport could provide that may be pertinent to its application, it provides some examples of information TSA has found useful and that airports could consider providing to TSA to help assess their suitability for the program. Further, the guidance, in combination with the description of the SPP application evaluation process, outlines how TSA plans to analyze and use cost information regarding screening cost efficiency and effectiveness. The guidance also states that providing cost information is optional and that not providing such information will not affect the application decision. As we reported in January 2014, these actions address the intent of our recommendation.

PERFORMANCE BETWEEN SPP AND NON-SPP AIRPORTS VARIED; TSA RECENTLY DEVELOPED A MECHANISM TO MONITOR PRIVATE VERSUS FEDERAL SCREENER PERFORMANCE

In our December 2012 report, we analyzed screener performance data for four measures and found that there were differences in performance between SPP and non-SPP airports, and those differences could not be exclusively attributed to the use of either Federal or private screeners. The four measures we selected to compare screener performance at SPP and non-SPP airports were Threat Image Projection (TIP) detection rates; recertification pass rates; Aviation Security Assessment Program (ASAP) test results; and Presence, Advisement, Communication, and Execution (PACE) evaluation results (see Table 1). For each of these four measures, we compared the performance of each of the 16 airports then participating in the SPP with the average performance for each airport's category (X, I, II, III, or IV), as well as the National performance averages for all airports for fiscal years 2009 through 2011.[13]

---

ciency of converting to the SPP because they did not have data on Federal screening costs, while the fourth airport operator did not need additional information or guidance to respond to the question. Further, three of the four airport operators we interviewed said that additional guidance would have been helpful in completing the application and determining how TSA evaluates the applications. See GAO–13–208 for more information.

[13] Additional information on these performance measures and how we selected them can be found in our December 2012 report. See GAO–13–208.

TABLE 1.—PERFORMANCE MEASURES USED TO COMPARE SCREENER PER-
FORMANCE AT SCREENING PARTNERSHIP PROGRAM (SPP) AND NON-SPP
AIRPORTS, DECEMBER 2012

Performance Measure	Description
Threat Image Projection (TIP) detection rates.	TIPs are fictional threat images (guns, knives, improvised explosive devices, etc.) superimposed onto carry-on baggage as it passes through the X-ray machine. While screening carry-on baggage, screeners identify that a potential threat has been spotted by selecting a "threat" button. If the identified image is a TIP, the X-ray machine informs the screener that the threat was fictional. Otherwise, a screener will search the bag, as the threat object may be real.
Recertification pass rates ...	In order to maintain their certification to screen passengers and baggage, all screeners (at both SPP and non-SPP airports) must pass several recertification tests on an annual basis. These tests include assessments of threat detection skills on carry-on and checked baggage X-ray machines as well as role-playing scenarios to assess other job functions, such as physical bag searches, pat-downs, and screening passengers with disabilities.
Aviation Security Assessment Program (ASAP) tests results.	ASAP tests are covert performance assessments conducted at both screening checkpoints and checked baggage screening areas. Tests are implemented locally by unrecognizable role players who attempt to pass standard test items, such as knives, guns, or simulated improvised explosive devices, through the screening checkpoints or checked baggage screening areas.
Presence, Advisement, Communication, and Execution (PACE) evaluations.	PACE evaluations are used to assess screener performance on various elements that may affect security and a passenger's overall traveling experience. PACE evaluators visit a checkpoint covertly and assess the screening personnel on a variety of elements, such as whether the officers provide comprehensive instruction and engage passengers in a calm and respectful manner when screening. Because PACE evaluations began as a baseline assessment program in fiscal year 2011 and had been implemented only at Category X, I, and II airports, our analysis for this measure was limited to the 6 SPP airports in those categories during fiscal year 2011.[1]

Source: GAO analysis of TSA information. GAO–14–787T.

[1] The 6 Category X, I, and II SPP airports in fiscal year 2011 are San Francisco International Airport (X), Kansas City International Airport (I), Greater Rochester International Airport (I), Key West International Airport (II), Joe Foss Field (II), and Jackson Hole Airport (II).

As we reported in December 2012, on the basis of our analyses, we found that, generally, screeners at certain SPP airports performed slightly above the airport category and National averages for some measures, while others performed slightly below. For example, at SPP airports, screeners performed above their respective airport category averages for recertification pass rates in the majority of instances, while at the majority of SPP airports that took PACE evaluations in 2011, screeners performed below their airport category averages.[14] For TIP detection rates, screeners at SPP airports performed above their respective airport category averages in about half of the instances. However, we also reported in December 2012 that the differences we observed in private and Federal screener performance cannot be en-

---

[14] For recertification pass rates, the term "instance" means performance by an airport during a particular year or fiscal year, while for TIP detection rates, the term means performance by an airport during a particular fiscal year for a specific type of screening machine.

tirely attributed to the type of screeners at an airport, because, according to TSA officials and other subject-matter experts, many factors, some of which cannot be controlled for, affect screener performance. These factors include, but are not limited to, checkpoint layout, airline schedules, seasonal changes in travel volume, and type of traveler.

We also reported in December 2012 that TSA collects data on several other performance measures but, for various reasons, the data cannot be used to compare private and Federal screener performance for the purposes of our review. For example, passenger wait time data could not be used because we found that TSA's policy for collecting wait times changed during the time period of our analyses and that these data were not collected in a consistent manner across all airports.[15] We also considered reviewing human capital measures such as attrition, absenteeism, and injury rates, but did not analyze these data because TSA's Office of Human Capital does not collect these data for SPP airports. We reported that while the contractors collect and report this information to the SPP PMO, TSA does not validate the accuracy of the self-reported data nor does it require contractors to use the same human capital measures as TSA, and accordingly, differences may exist in how the metrics are defined and how the data are collected. Therefore, we found that TSA could not guarantee that a comparison of SPP and non-SPP airports on these human capital metrics would be an equal comparison.

Moreover, in December 2012, we found that while TSA monitored screener performance at all airports, the agency did not monitor private screener performance separately from Federal screener performance or conduct regular reviews comparing the performance of SPP and non-SPP airports. Beginning in April 2012, TSA introduced a new set of performance measures to assess screener performance at all airports (both SPP and non-SPP) in its Office of Security Operations Executive Scorecard (the Scorecard). Officials told us at the time of our December 2012 review that they provided the Scorecard to FSDs every 2 weeks to assist the FSDs with tracking performance against stated goals and with determining how performance of the airports under their jurisdiction compared with National averages.[16] According to TSA, the 10 measures used in the Scorecard were selected based on input from FSDs and regional directors on the performance measures that most adequately reflected screener and airport performance.[17] Performance measures in the Scorecard included the TIP detection rate and the number of negative and positive customer contacts made to the TSA Contact Center through e-mails or phone calls per 100,000 passengers screened, among others.[18]

We also reported in December 2012 that TSA had conducted or commissioned prior reports comparing the cost and performance of SPP and non-SPP airports. For example, in 2004 and 2007, TSA commissioned reports prepared by private consultants, while in 2008 the agency issued its own report comparing the performance of SPP and non-SPP airports.[19] Generally, these reports found that SPP airports performed at a level equal to or better than non-SPP airports. However, TSA officials stated at the time that they did not plan to conduct similar analyses in the future, and instead, they were using across-the-board mechanisms of both private and Fed-

---

[15] TSA's policy for measuring wait time changed in March 2010. Instead of collecting precise wait times every hour, TSA began only recording instances in which the wait time was more than 20 or 30 minutes. Further, through our site visits conducted for the December 2012 report, we learned that TSA collects airports' wait time data in different ways. For example, at some airports TSA calculates the wait time from the end of the queue until the passenger reaches the travel document checker podium; at other airports, TSA calculates the time from the end of the line until the passenger passes through the walkthrough metal detector or the Advanced Imaging Technology. See GAO–13–208.

[16] Although FSDs provide day-to-day operational direction for security operations at the airports within their jurisdiction, including those participating in the SPP, FSDs have responsibility for overall security at SPP airports but do not have direct control over workforce management. Rather, the SPP contractor is contractually obligated to effectively and efficiently manage its screening workforce.

[17] Prior to the Scorecard, from 2006 through April 2012, FSDs used three performance measures in the Management Objective Report (MOR) to assess screener and airport performance. The MOR included three measures that assessed screener performance, including TIP detection rates, Advanced Imaging Technology checkpoint utilization, and layered security effectiveness. For more on these performance measures, see GAO–13–208.

[18] The TSA Contact Center handles these customer contacts for all of TSA, not only those related to passenger and baggage screening. For more on the Scorecard performance measures, see GAO–13–208.

[19] Bearing Point, Inc., *Private Screening Operations Performance Evaluation Report* (Apr. 16, 2004); Catapult Consultants, LLC, *Private Screening Operations: Business Case Analysis, Transportation Security Administration, Screening Partnership Program* (Arlington, Virginia: Dec. 14, 2007); and TSA, *A Report on SPP Airport Cost and Performance Analysis and Comparison to Business Case Analysis Finding* (Arlington, Virginia: Feb. 1, 2008).

eral screeners, such as the Scorecard, to assess screener performance across all commercial airports.

We found that in addition to using the Scorecard, TSA conducted monthly contractor performance management reviews (PMR) at each SPP airport to assess the contractor's performance against the standards set in each SPP contract. The PMRs included 10 performance measures, including some of the same measures included in the Scorecard, such as TIP detection rates and recertification pass rates, for which TSA establishes acceptable quality levels of performance. Failure to meet the acceptable quality levels of performance could result in corrective actions or termination of the contract.

However, in December 2012, we found that the Scorecard and PMR did not provide a complete picture of screener performance at SPP airports because, while both mechanisms provided a snapshot of private screener performance at each SPP airport, this information was not summarized for the SPP as a whole or across years, which made it difficult to identify changes in performance. Further, neither the Scorecard nor the PMR provided information on performance in prior years or controlled for variables that TSA officials explained to us were important when comparing private and Federal screener performance, such as the type of X-ray machine used for TIP detection rates. We concluded that monitoring private screener performance in comparison with Federal screener performance was consistent with the statutory requirement that TSA enter into a contract with a private screening company only if the administrator determines and certifies to Congress that the level of screening services and protection provided at an airport under a contract will be equal to or greater than the level that would be provided at the airport by Federal Government personnel.[20] Therefore, we recommended that TSA develop a mechanism to regularly monitor private versus Federal screener performance, which would better position the agency to know whether the level of screening services and protection provided at SPP airports continues to be equal to or greater than the level provided at non-SPP airports.

TSA concurred with the recommendation, and has taken actions to address it. Specifically, in January 2013, TSA issued its first SPP Annual Report. The report highlights the accomplishments of the SPP during fiscal year 2012 and provides an overview and discussion of private versus Federal screener cost and performance. The report also describes the criteria TSA used to select certain performance measures and reasons why other measures were not selected for its comparison of private and Federal screener performance. The report compares the performance of SPP airports with the average performance of airports in their respective category, as well as the average performance for all airports, for three performance measures: TIP detection rates, recertification pass rates, and PACE evaluation results. Further, in September 2013, the TSA assistant administrator for security operations signed an operations directive that provides internal guidance for preparing the SPP Annual Report, including the requirement that the SPP PMO must annually verify that the level of screening services and protection provided at SPP airports is equal to or greater than the level that would be provided by Federal screeners. We believe that these actions address the intent of our recommendation and should better position TSA to determine whether the level of screening services and protection provided at SPP airports continues to be equal to or greater than the level provided at non-SPP airports. Further, these actions could also assist TSA in identifying performance changes that could lead to improvements in the program and inform decision making regarding potential expansion of the SPP.

TSA CONTINUES TO ADDRESS LIMITATIONS IN THE METHODOLOGY FOR COMPARING THE COSTS OF SPP AND NON-SPP SCREENING SERVICES

TSA has faced challenges in accurately comparing the costs of screening services at SPP and non-SPP airports. In 2007, TSA estimated that SPP airports would cost about 17 percent more to operate than airports using Federal screeners. In our January 2009 report we noted strengths in the methodology's design, but also identified seven limitations in TSA's methodology that could affect the accuracy and reliability of cost comparisons, and its usefulness in informing future management decisions.[21]

---

[20] See 49 U.S.C. § 44920(d) (providing further that private screening companies must be owned and controlled by a citizen of the United States, subject to a waiver of this requirement by the TSA administrator in certain circumstances).

[21] TSA's study design: (1) Did not consider the impact of overlapping administrative personnel on the costs of SPP airports; (2) underestimated costs to the Government for non-SPP airports by not including all costs associated with providing passenger and baggage screening services; (3) included more uncertainty in the cost estimates for non-SPP airports than for SPP airports,

Continued

58

We recommended that if TSA planned to rely on its comparison of cost and performance of SPP and non-SPP airports for future decision making, the agency should update its analysis to address the limitations we identified. TSA generally concurred
with our findings and recommendation. In March 2011, TSA provided us with an
update on the status of its efforts to address the limitations we cited in our report,
as well as a revised comparison of costs for screening operations at SPP and non-
SPP airports. This revised cost comparison generally addressed three of the seven
limitations and provided TSA with a more reasonable basis for comparing the
screening cost at SPP and non-SPP airports. In the update, TSA estimated that SPP
airports would cost 3 percent more to operate in 2011 than airports using Federal
screeners. In March 2011, we found that TSA had also taken actions that partially
addressed the four remaining limitations related to cost, but needed to take additional actions or provide additional documentation. In July 2014, TSA officials stated they are continuing to make additional changes to the cost estimation methodology and we are continuing to monitor TSA's progress in this area through on-going
work.

Chairman Hudson, Ranking Member Richmond, and Members of the subcommittee, this completes my prepared statement. I would be happy to respond to
any questions you may have at this time.

Mr. HUDSON. Thank you, Ms. Grover.

We appreciate you both being here today.

I now recognize myself for 5 minutes to ask questions.

Mr. Benner, according to TSA's cost comparison of SPP versus
non-SPP airports last year, which one was less expensive and by
what percentage?

Mr. BENNER. The overall average for last year, SPP airports were
approximately 2 percent less—0.2 percent less, excuse me, than
non-SPP airports. But I do want to mention, as Ms. Grover mentioned, that there really is a point in time. That could change between airport to airport, because some airports are a little higher,
some airports are a little lower. That also could change year over
year based on a number of different variables, just as one example
is as TSA on the Federal side is reaping the benefits of the RBS
program, it takes just a little bit longer through contract modifications to reap the same benefits on the SPP side of the house.

So, any given year, you are going to have a little bit of a difference between the cost between SPP and non-SPP. If we had a
very static environment that we worked in, then the cost would remain relatively the same cost comparison, but we don't, we have
a fluid environment.

Mr. HUDSON. Can you explain the methodology and sort-of the
specific elements used to produce your cost comparison?

Mr. BENNER. Are you talking about the FCEs, sir?

Mr. HUDSON. Sure.

Mr. BENNER. So included in the FCE are all the actual costs at
an airport and the benefits; so the actual wages at the airport, the
actual benefits at the airport, less those that are not paid by TSA.
For instance, TSA includes in its Federal cost estimate the retirement cost that TSA actually pays into the system.

59

What it does not include, however, are the unfunded retirement liabilities that are not paid by TSA; they are actually paid by OPM. So that entire Federal cost estimate does include all costs for which TSA is appropriated funds in one form or another for that particular airport.

Mr. HUDSON. Well, do you agree if you are not adding the retirement costs into the comparison that SPP airports actually would be even more cost-effective than what the current comparison seems to show?

Mr. BENNER. Sir, not necessarily. Because what would happen if we included—hypothetically, if we were to include the unfunded retirement liability, and there are a couple other minor imputed costs that we don't cover as well. We would probably have to include those costs in the bottom line ATSA rate, which is paid, for instance, that would increase that ATSA rate as the floor that TSOs are actually paid so it would also increase that. So the relative distance between the ceiling and the floor would remain probably relatively stable.

Mr. HUDSON. I might follow up with you on that later.

I want to get to the next question. I am sure you heard the first panel. A lot of concerns were raised. Ultimately, it is your responsibility to address the stakeholder concerns so I want to give you an opportunity to respond to some of these. Just to summarize, the airports were not being kept in the loop during the contracting process was one. Companies were frustrated with TSA's cost methodology, which we touched on here. The process of awarding contracts takes far too long, and there is skepticism about the validity of TSA's best-value analysis of SPP proposals. How confident are you that TSA is selecting the bast value proposal on evaluating SPP bids as opposed to simply selecting the lowest price offer?

Mr. BENNER. Is there a particular place you want me to start there?

Mr. HUDSON. Yeah, that was a lot. Starting with I guess evaluating SPP bids.

Mr. BENNER. If I might, Mr. Chairman, I did listen to the comments of the previous panel, and I do have to say that being in charge of the SPP program, having been in the position now for 6½, 7 months, I kind of take it personally. I feel badly if is there is a perception that the reason that folks aren't participating in the program is because of something we are doing wrong.

I think we have had a lot of improvements in the SPP program, particularly within the last couple of years. Are we perfect? Absolutely not. Are we getting better? I am convinced we are. So, just as an example, since the FAA Modernization Act, Congress has stipulated we had 120 days to approve an application. What we have done within TSA, and I think our administrator testified to this earlier and then our system administrator in January of this year, that we have set our own internal goal to process all the way from application to contract award, assuming that we can find a qualified vendor within 12 months.

That is a very aggressive time line, given the fact that we have to follow all the requirements of the Federal Acquisition Regulation, but I think it is a reflection of our commitment to try to do this and do it right.

60

Some of the problems that we have had in the past, surely some
of them we have owned, and we have had some missteps. But also
some was calculated decisions based on if there was new legislation
that came out, and we felt—for instance, with the FAA Modernization Act, that we weren't meeting the strict requirements of the
new legislation, then we decided to take a pause, take those procurement actions that were actually out there in the procurement
phase, pull them back and make sure that we were in compliance
with the new legislation before we put them back out again.

Sometimes this would take a year or 2 in order to turn everything—turn all those procurements around and get them out there
again. I have a little bit different mind-set in that I think that if
we have a procurement action that is out there and we have a
slight change in legislation or there a slight change in report via
report from Congress, that the first thing we should be doing is
checking with Congress to say, do you really want us to hold up
or can we continue on with the current methodology and then when
we go to the next round of procurements, integrate that?

That is actually what we did during for the 2014 appropriations
report. We actually checked with the appropriations staff to see if
they wanted us to hold fast with some of the guidance I had in the
report or continue on with the appropriations that we had on-going.
The consensus was, keep moving, but wait until the independent
study is done, that is on-going right now, and then make any necessary changes after that. I am sorry, I hope that answered your
question.

Mr. HUDSON. I didn't give you enough time to answer it completely. But I appreciate that very much.

My time has expired. At this point, I will recognize the
gentlelady from Texas, Ms. Jackson Lee, for any questions she may
have.

Ms. JACKSON LEE. Mr. Chairman, thank you so very much and
thank you for this hearing, I thank my colleagues, and thank Mr.
Richmond as well, and to the witnesses to the previous panel that
I know is already gone. I am in the middle of another hearing
which I will have to depart for, but I know this is very important.

I want to thank the two witnesses, Ms. Grover for her testimony
and Mr. Benner for his testimony.

Let me pursue the issue—you made a point so let me just quickly
raise the point. We really don't have a refined assessment of
whether the SPP program is less expensive. Is that correct? We
can't really stand on the table and bang on the table and say, that
is the case.

Mr. BENNER. Ma'am, we have an assessment methodology that
we can compare SPP and non-SPP airports. What I was trying to
say is that we can't say that that difference between SPP and non-
SPP airports is going to remain the same year over year.

Ms. JACKSON LEE. Right, and I understand that. What I am saying is we could not make a declarative, firm, final statement that
one is less expensive than the other or the SPP is less expensive
than the other approach.

Mr. BENNER. Correct.

Ms. JACKSON LEE. Thank you very much.

I want to know, Mr. Benner, TSA recently sent a letter to the Department of Labor stating that the agency was not considering prevailing wage requirements in SPP contracts, despite a directive of the Labor's wage and hour division instructing TSA to do so. Will you now reassess that and actually go back and look at requiring prevailing wages for those workers?

Mr. BENNER. Ma'am, I understand a letter went out a couple of weeks ago. As recently as yesterday, there has been some discussion within the Executive branch or a number of different agencies involved to talk about the legal and policy—have a legal and policy discussion concerning the relationship between ATSA and SCA.

I think between Department of Homeland Security, Department of Labor, and TSA, those discussions are on-going right now, so it would be a little premature for me to have any declarative statement at this point.

Ms. JACKSON LEE. Well, let me try to help you out in getting a more firm statement. There is a lot of discussions. Is it your understanding that DHS, TSA is reconsidering a decision that did not utilize prevailing wages with all the discussions going on, and in actuality, those are discussions that are now going on are to discuss the utilization of prevailing wages?

Mr. BENNER. Ma'am, I don't know that TSA and DHS are reconsidering. I do know that there are discussions on-going, and there will be a resolution at some point as to what the position will be for the Executive branch.

Ms. JACKSON LEE. Are you engaged in those discussions which do not advocate for including the prevailing wage?

Mr. BENNER. No, those discussions principally within TSA are on-going between our Office of Acquisitions, which is principally responsible for instituting the SCA, and our legal department.

Ms. JACKSON LEE. Okay. So can I understand from your testimony that the issue utilizing the prevailing wage is now being considered or discussed at this time?

Mr. BENNER. It is being discussed, yes, ma'am.

Ms. JACKSON LEE. Let me offer to say that I think that is a very important point for the competency and quality of the individuals. I've always raised the question of the adequacy of privatizing the security of our airports, pre-9/11 and post-9/11, and I know this is your responsibility, and I thank you for the work you are doing.

This is not a critiquing of your work. It is to say to my colleagues that I stand firm in opposition to privatizing and you have made the record today by saying you cannot determine whether there is any, if you will, cost savings at all. I would never suggest that any airport is on the cheap, but if you wanted to use that kind of language, and I am not going to use that kind of language, you would make the argument that, why do it that way, except for the fact that some airports have been grandfathered in?

I accept the grandfathering. I want to make that very clear. But going forward, I think you have all that you can handle and that we should in fact be able to do it in a different way.

Mr. Chairman, before I end, I would like to ask unanimous consent that testimony provided to the committee by John L. Martin, airport director of San Francisco International Airport, calling for TSA to comply with the Service Contract Act, SCA, and honor the current collectively bargaining rates of wages and benefits for its employees, be entered into the record. I ask unanimous consent.

Mr. HUDSON. Without objection.

[The information follows:]

STATEMENT OF JOHN L. MARTIN, AIRPORT DIRECTOR, SAN FRANCISCO INTERNATIONAL AIRPORT

JULY 29, 2014

Thank you for the opportunity to provide written testimony regarding the Transportation Security Administration's (TSA) management of the Screening Partnership Program (SPP). San Francisco International Airport (SFO) has been an "opt out" airport since 2002, when the original airport pilot program authorized in the Aviation Transportation Security Act (ATSA) was implemented.

In order to maintain the highest levels of safety and security, as well as continuing with a stable and experienced workforce and excellent customer service, SPP bid parameters for SFO should include the following:

- Honor current collective bargained rates of wages and benefits.
- Implement a Cost Plus Fixed Fee contract, the competition for which would remove wages as a bid item and focus on the qualifications of the management firm and its fees.

Twelve years since the "opt-out" program started, the TSA's original private screening contractor, Covenant Aviation Security (CAS), continues to provide screening services at SFO. Importantly, a large percentage of the original starting screener workforce at SFO continues to work for CAS under TSA supervision.

A core philosophy at SFO is teamwork and collaboration. From the inception of the SPP there has been a partnership approach comprised of TSA, CAS, SFO, and the union representing the workers, Service Employees International Union (SEIU). This team has developed a strong working relationship, creating a stable and secure workforce across all airport operations, enhancing our ability to maintain a safe and secure environment for the public and passengers. The dynamic environment of a large hub airport like SFO is extremely complicated and the ability to enhance teamwork and maintain a stable workforce through high retention rates is a key to our collective success.

According to the recently-released Request for Information (RFI) from TSA, the Agency plans to issue an RFP on August 14 of this year. The contract for screening services at SFO will be for a 1-year term with four 1-year options to extend. My primary concern is that the contract will be a fixed price with a "not to exceed ceiling" which may be based on TSA's entry-level minimum loaded wage rate factored for San Francisco. This rate may be lower than both CAS's current starting level rate and the average rate for the long-time employees who have been on the job at SFO for many years.

This lower threshold may incentivize bidders to assume the lowest available wage rate—the entry-level Federal screener rate. Our preferred approach would be to remove the wage rates from the competitive process and instead focus the selection on safety and security qualifications. TSA could also focus on competitive management fees.

Another troubling aspect of the RFP for screening services at SFO is the contract term of 1 year with four 1-year options to extend which could theoretically allow TSA to reset the wages and benefits several times during the next 5 years. This creates instability in the workforce and a strong element of uncertainty going forward. SFO is a major international gateway hub and we seek out the most qualified, skilled contractors available. It is essential that we create a stable work environment to ensure safety and security.

Our concerns, particularly with respect to the wage rates, would be addressed, in part, if the TSA followed the Service Contract Act (SCA). The TSA, however, has concluded that under ATSA it has the authority to establish wage rates for Federal screeners and is therefore exempt from the SCA. The SCA generally applies to every contract entered into by the Federal Government that has a principle purpose of furnishing services in the United States through the use of service employees. The SCA requires that Federal contracts include provisions setting forth minimum monetary wages and fringe benefits for the service employees in accordance with the prevailing rates for such employees in the locality.

The incumbent provider CAS has negotiated a Collective Bargaining Agreement (CBA) with SEIU, which would, in every other Federal service contract, automatically trigger prevailing wage requirements. By not following the SCA, the TSA would lower the wage and benefit rates which are then factored into the "not to exceed ceiling" costs. This interpretation of the ATSA could prohibit the incumbent and other potential competitors from bidding on the RFP for screening services at SFO as the CBA establishes wage and benefit rates higher than TSA's entry-level wage and benefit packages.

This effort by TSA to restrain costs to the SPP program would require the contract awarded in all likelihood to reduce the wages of the current workforce by up to 15–20%. This loss of wages by the current workforce would be disruptive, unfair, and difficult to manage. To my knowledge, TSA is not attempting to re-set the wages of Federal screeners at any other airport.

In closing, I urge the TSA to carefully consider the parameters of the SPP RFP for SFO to ensure a stable and productive workforce by honoring the current collective bargained rates of wages and benefits and implementing a Cost Plus Fixed Fee contact, the competition for which would remove wages as a bid item and focus on the qualifications of the management firm and its fees.

We look forward to supporting TSA in this process.

Ms. JACKSON LEE. I ask, additionally, Mr. Chairman, I ask unanimous consent to enter into the record testimony provided to the committee from Valarie Long, executive vice president of Service Employees International Union, which expresses serious concerns about the failure of TSA to comply with the Department of Labor decision on service contracts and points to the fundamental problem to public security that arises when employees, Federal or contracted, are not adequately trained and compensated. I ask unanimous consent.

Mr. HUDSON. Without objection, so ordered.

[The information follows:]

STATEMENT OF VALARIE LONG, EXECUTIVE VICE PRESIDENT, SERVICE EMPLOYEES INTERNATIONAL UNION (SEIU)

JULY 29, 2014

Thank you Chairman Hudson, Ranking Member Richmond, and Members of the subcommittee for the opportunity to submit written testimony for today's hearing examining the Transportation Security Administration's (TSA) management of the Screening Partnership Program. My name is Valarie Long, executive vice president of the Service Employees International Union, representing more than 250,000 workers across North America who clean, maintain, and provide security for commercial office buildings, co-ops, and apartment buildings, as well as public facilities like theaters, stadiums, and airports. I am pleased to submit testimony on behalf of the more 1,100 private security screeners at San Francisco International Airport (SFO), represented by SEIU-United Service Workers West and employed by Covenant Aviation Security.

We are writing to share our serious concerns about TSA's failure to abide by a Department of Labor ruling that the Service Contract Act (SCA) applies to security contracts entered into as part of the Screening Partnership Program, and to provide the subcommittee with detailed information about the potential threat this decision may pose to passengers and personnel at SFO. Our view has long been that whether the work is performed by direct Federal employees or by contract employees, screeners should be adequately trained and compensated to ensure we retain their abilities to protect passengers and the public.

SFO: A PARTNERSHIP FOR QUALITY

The private security screeners at SFO may wear different uniform insignia than screeners employed by TSA, but these brave men and women selflessly serve our country. They have been proud union members since 2000 when we helped launch SFO's Quality Standards Program (QSP), a partnership between the city of San Francisco, the Airport Commission, private contractors and unions representing SFO workers. QSP was designed to improve safety and security at SFO as well as improve the conditions of the SFO labor market, by establishing compensation, recruitment, and training standards beyond those then-required by the FAA, for a wide range of airport employees.[1]

Since its inception in 2000, QSP has succeeded in its goal of producing a stable, experienced, quality screener workforce. Prior to its launch, screeners' wages were low and the turnover rate among was high. By 9/11, just 17 months after program implementation began in April 2000—and at the moment when the rest of the world learned of the tragic effects of low-road contracted-out screening—the annual turnover rate of SFO security screeners plummeted from 110 percent in 1999 to about 25 percent.[2] Turnover rates continued to decline; a 2003 study of security screeners at SFO found that the turnover rate continued dropping to 18.7 percent.[3] In addition to lower turnover rates, airport employers at SFO reported improved overall work performance (35%), better employee morale (47%), fewer disciplinary issues (44%), and improved customer service (45%) in the first year of the living wage law, a key feature of the QSP.[4]

As a result of QSP, the SFO screener workforce has been recognized for excellent performance, high morale—which reduces absenteeism and increases willingness to adapt flexibly—and quality customer service.[5] According to researchers, "[o]ne of the main advantages of the SFO program is the breadth of its impact. By linking wage improvements to training and accreditation programs, the program has gone a long way to improving morale and performance across the entire airport."[6]

In the years since 2000 screeners and their employers at SFO have bargained collectively to improve wages, benefits, and working conditions. Our current estimate of turnover among the full-time screener workforce at SFO is 2.8 percent and average experience over 4.8 years. This compares to a turnover rate among full-time TSA screeners of between 12 and 13 percent in 2013.[7] Taken as a whole, the workforce at SFO has 3,619 person-years of experience.

ONE SCREENER'S STORY

Euell Lim has served as a Transportation Security Officer (TSO) at SFO since 2009, where he applies the security standards of the Federal Government to properly screen passengers onto their flight. "I follow strict standard operating procedures," he says, "as a passenger goes through the security checkpoint, and to be able to provide customer service which is very important."

Learning the job has been a process, Euell says, "like when you go to school. We're not going to graduate in a week, a month, or a year . . . It's a learning process and that takes time." There is "a huge gap between one who's experienced and one who's just starting. There are mistakes that can be done if they're not trained properly, if they're not attended to." Fortunately, Euell was "blessed" with a great training mentor, a senior employee who "was very attentive and very specific and very detail-minded." And behind the mentor was a good support system and a great training staff.

For Euell, the passengers are the beneficiaries of his training. "There's a sense of security. There's a sense of respect. The way you conduct yourself in a professional manner, done by proper training. You earn the respect of the traveling public . . . And I think just to be able to absorb that time with passengers and

[1] Michael Reich, Peter Hall, and Ken Jacobs, "Living Wages and Economic Performance: The San Francisco Airport Model," Institute of Industrial Relations, University of California, Berkeley, 2003, http://laborcenter.berkeley.edu/livingwage/living_wage_performance.pdf.
[2] Living Wages and Airport Security. Preliminary report. Michael Reich, Peter Hall, Ken Jacobs, Institute of Labor and Employment. University of California, Berkeley, September 20, 2001, p. 5. http://www.irle.berkeley.edu/research/livingwage/air_sep01.pdf.
[3] Living Wages and Economic Performance: The San Francisco Airport Model. Michael Reich, Peter Hall, Ken Jacobs, Institute of Industrial Relations at the University of California, Berkeley, March 2003; and Aviation Security: Long Standing Problems Impair Airport Screeners' Performance. GAO. June 2000, p. 25.
[4] Living Wages and Economic Performance: The San Francisco Airport Model. Michael Reich, Peter Hall, Ken Jacobs, Institute of Industrial Relations at the University of California, Berkeley, March 2003. http://www.irle.berkeley.edu/research/livingwage/sfo_mar03.pdf.
[5] Michael Reich, Peter Hall, and Ken Jacobs, "Living Wages and Economic Performance: The San Francisco Airport Model," Institute of Industrial Relations, University of California, Berkeley (2003). http://www.irle.berkeley.edu/research/livingwage/sfo_mar03.pdf.
[6] Living Wages and Airport Security. Preliminary report. Michael Reich, Peter Hall, Ken Jacobs, Institute of Labor and Employment. University of California, Berkeley, September 20, 2001, p. 6. http://www.irle.berkeley.edu/research/livingwage/air_sep01.pdf.
[7] According to the testimony of Mr. Kelly Hoggan, Assistant Administrator for Security Operations, TSA "TSA Oversight: Examining the Screening Partnership Program," House Committee on Oversight and Government Reform, Subcommittee on Government Operations, January 14, 2015.

being able to have the right positive experiences, can contribute to something more constructive."

Euell's hourly wage is $22.01, which allows him "a little bit more freedom than other people I'm aware of who work in the airport. I'm able to pay off my credit card, my bills. I'm able to provide for my son." His wage provides something intangible, but equally important,

"I'm almost forty and from my experiences in life, on the jobs I've worked, and the hats that I've worn throughout my life, I feel that earning a respectable wage and comfortable living is within everyone's right to function in our society. Just to have a little bit of self-respect, and to provide the respect for my family and children. Being a part of what I do here, I feel I have a significant role in defending and providing the dignity and respect for the coworkers that I have grown to be accustomed to."

Euell Lim bears testament to the palpable advances in the quality of screening made at SFO over the last 15 years.

SFO'S EXPERIENCED WORKFORCE AT RISK AS A RESULT OF TSA'S FAILURE TO COMPLY WITH THE SERVICE CONTRACT ACT

Unfortunately, we understand that TSA has held that the Service Contract Act's (SCA) prevailing wage standards do not apply to private security screening contracts, despite being directed to do so by the Department of Labor's Wage and Hour Division.[8] The McNamara-O'Hara Service Contract Act requires contractors and subcontractors performing services on prime contracts in excess of $2,500 to pay service employees in various classes no less than the wage rates and fringe benefits found prevailing in the locality, or the rates (including prospective increases) contained in a predecessor contractor's collective bargaining agreement.[9] At SFO this would mean that the economic provisions of the CBA would continue, regardless of who wins a contract to provide security screening services.

On June 6, 2013, the Department of Labor's Wage and Hour Division issued an opinion that the Service Contract Act applies to all private security screening contracts entered into by TSA, and directed TSA "to take all necessary steps to ensure the applicable contracts contain the SCA's prevailing wage standards."[10] TSA responded earlier this month that SCA standards do not apply.[11]

TSA's failure to apply SCA standards to the security contracts at SFO will erode the quality advancements made and significantly undermine this highly-trained workforce. TSA's refusal to apply the SCA will likely result in significant wage reductions for SFO screeners. In the absence of SCA standards, and if a contractor follows TSA's recommendation and bids at TSA minimum direct labor rates,[12] wages for virtually all screeners at SFO could be cut from 7% to as much as 27%. For example,

- Lead Screeners and CTX 9000 Specialists, currently earning $62,649.60 would suffer a nearly 27% cut ($16,748.61);
- Beginning Screeners and CTX Operators, currently earning $43,097.60 would suffer a 19% cut ($8,265.39);
- Screeners and CTX Operators with 10 years or more longevity, currently earning $47,507.20 would suffer a 26% cut ($12,674.99);
- Behavior Detection Officers currently earning $49,316.80 would suffer a 7% wage cut ($3,415.81);

[8] See Letter from Timothy J. Helm, Chief, Branch of Government Contracts Enforcement, Division of Enforcement Policy and Procedures, Wage and Hour Division, U.S. Department of Labor, to Francine Kerner, Chief Counsel, Transportation Security Administration, June 6, 2013; and Letter from Ronald B. Gallihugh, Head of the Contracting Activity, Transportation Security Administration, to Timothy J. Helm, Chief, Branch of Government Contracts Enforcement, Wage and Hour Division, U.S. Department of Labor, July 3, 2014.

[9] 41 U.S.C. 6703(1).

[10] Letter from Timothy J. Helm, Chief, Branch of Government Contracts Enforcement, Division of Enforcement Policy and Procedures, Wage and Hour Division, U.S. Department of Labor, to Francine Kerner, Chief Counsel, Transportation Security Administration, June 6, 2013.

[11] TSA does accept SCA applicability to clerical staff associated with SPP contracts. Under the Aviation and Transportation Security Act of 2002 (ATSA). Letter from Ronald B. Gallihugh, Head of the Contracting Activity, Transportation Security Administration, to Timothy J. Helm, Chief, Branch of Government Contracts Enforcement, Wage and Hour Division, U.S. Department of Labor, July 3, 2014.

[12] See, for example, "Airport Security Screening Services at MCI [Kansas City International Airport], *Solicitation Number: HSTS05-12-R-SPP038*, Department of Homeland Security, Transportation Security Administration, p. 81. For TSA recommendations to prospective bidders, see: *Amendment 3 Mod/Amendment: FINAL-MCI QandA[1] Description: Attached are the questions and answers submitted in response to HSTS05-12-R-SPP038.*

- Of the 150 full-time employees who are at or above TSA's Pay Band F:
  - 108 have at least 2 years' experience.
  - Of these, 61 Lead Screeners and CTX 9000 Specialists have 10 years or more experience.
- Of the 561 full-time employees at or above TSA's Pay Band D for TSO:
  - 521 have at least 3 years' experience.
  - Of these, 168 have 10 years or more experience.[13]

Ensuring SCA requirements apply to private screening contracts is the best way to retain the high standards for screeners built at SFO. However, if TSA is permitted to disregard the findings of the Department of Labor that the Service Contract Act applies to private screeners, prospective bidders could massively undercut the wages of the screener workforce at SFO. And the largest cuts would fall disproportionately on those workers—like Euell—with the most experience. This is precisely the workforce TSA should strive to retain.

Workers are profoundly wage-sensitive, and cuts of this magnitude would be deeply painful—to themselves and to the passengers and public whom they serve. These workers would have many employment options, given their seniority and the prevailing wages elsewhere in San Francisco's security industry; many would likely leave the job, taking their critical skills and experience with them.

Such a massive loss of talent at SFO, as experienced officers leave for employment elsewhere, could have a potentially catastrophic impact on the quality of service. The importance of retaining quality screeners was one of the 9/11 Commission's important findings. The commission found that one potential hijacker was turned back as he tried to enter the United States by an immigration inspector who relied on intuitive experience to ask questions. "Good people who have worked in such jobs for a long time understand this phenomenon well," the commission found,

"Other evidence we obtained confirmed the importance of letting experienced gate agents or security screeners ask questions and use their judgment. This is not an invitation to arbitrary exclusions. But any effective system has to grant some scope, perhaps in a little extra inspection or one more check, to the instincts and discretion of well-trained human beings."[14]

The importance of experience was again demonstrated during the November 1, 2013 attack at LAX which took the life of TSA Officer Gerardo Hernandez. Two other officers were also shot by the perpetrator, yet despite their wounds, continued to help people to safety:[15] Officer Tony Grigsby, a Master Behavior Detection Officer (MBDO), started at TSA in 2004. Officer James Speer, a Master Security Training Instructor, joined TSA in 2008.

Application of the Service Contract Act to the screener workforce, which would require bidders to incorporate the wage rates and fringe benefits contained in a predecessor contractor's collective bargaining agreement, would be the most effective means to ensure the retention of the experienced, quality private screener workforce at SFO.

CONCLUSION

This workforce is the product of the deliberate decision made in 2000 by the city of San Francisco, the Airport Commission, and representative unions to form the Quality Services Program. While it took more than a decade to build it, the work-

---

[13] Methodological discussion: *Wage Comparison.*—(1) At SFO, Covenant Aviation Security (CAS) employs SFO security workers in specific CAS Titles and CAS Steps defined by collective bargaining agreement (CBA). For each position held, the CAS Hourly wage rate was multiplied by 2080 hours (TSA's standard for a non-leap year) to produce the CAS Annual Wage. (2) TSA wages were calculated based on the Wage Determination for Screeners (2012–07–23 TSA–MCI Solicitation 1 HSTS05–12–R–SPP038, p. 81). That is, the 2014 minimum annual direct labor rates for Pay Band D and Pay Band F, respectively, adjusted for Locality Pay (35.15%). *Experience.*—(1) CAS provided the number of workers in each CAS Title and CAS Step, as defined by the CBA. In most cases, the title and step define the minimum experience necessary to hold that position. The years of experience defined by title and step were multiplied by the number of persons holding that position to produce CAS Full Time Experience, expressed in person-years. (a) Because the CBA does not define steps between 3 and 10 years of experience, the actual experience of SFO security screeners is likely to be substantially higher. (b) For positions corresponding to TSA Pay Band F (Lead Screener, CTX Lead, or CTX 9000 Specialist), even those workers indicated as having zero (0) years of experience in that position probably have substantial relevant experience. In general, workers enter these positions after having experience in positions corresponding to TSA Pay Band D (Screener or CTX Operator).

[14] Report, National Commission on Terrorist Attacks Upon the United States," July 22, 2004, p. 387.

[15] See, "Honoring Our Fallen TSO," November 8, 2013, posted by Transportation Security Administration Administrator John Pistole.

67

force could be destroyed very rapidly. And it would be extremely difficult—if not impossible—to recreate it. On behalf of the more than 1,100 security screeners at SFO, I urge you to ensure that this dedicated, highly-trained, and skilled workforce can continue to provide the safe and secure airport experience on which passengers depend. I ask that you take every effort to ensure that TSA and the Screening Partnership Program are in compliance with the requirements of the Service Contract Act. Thank you for the opportunity to submit written testimony on the Screening Partnership Program and the continued successes at San Francisco International Airport.

Ms. JACKSON LEE. I thank the Chairman.

I thank the witnesses for your very important testimony.

I yield back, Mr. Chairman.

Mr. HUDSON. I thank the gentlelady.

This time, the Chairman recognizes the gentleman from South Carolina, Mr. Sanford, for any questions he may have.

Mr. SANFORD. Thank you, Mr. Chairman.

It just strikes me that in analyzing any program, the bottom line is in part driven by results. So if I could, just in terms of giving broad, broad picture, with the SPP program, what percentage of all airports out there are under Federal contract versus private contract?

Mr. BENNER. We have 18 airports that are under private contract, out of 450 total airports.

Mr. SANFORD. Yeah, but they may be minuscule in Montana and—nothing against Montana, but with one employee. I mean, how about overall employees?

Mr. BENNER. We don't measure the SPP airports by number of employees. But perhaps I can explain it by saying that about 4.5 percent of all passenger throughput through the U.S. aviation system is through SPP airports. I think that's probably a fair way to look at it.

Mr. SANFORD. So that would be 4.5 percent of all airports, but that may not take into consideration overall hours worked, number of employees at those airports.

With most programs out there, if you said: Look, you know, 96 percent or 95 percent of it is being done one way and 5 percent is being done this other way, you would say well, it is sort of a rounding error. You have three standard deviations in the world of statistics, and you are still at sort of zero. So it is sound of a rounding error for lack of a better term.

It just strikes me to the linchpin of the reason it is a rounding error I think is in large part tied to what the Chairman was just getting at in the cost differential. It still seems to me that it is not a really robust competition given the fact that you are taking out a lot of what any Federal worker would rightfully consider the package of benefits that go with Federal employment, and that is retirement and so associated benefits. How can that be a real competition? I think the numbers suggest it is not a real competition.

Mr. BENNER. Well, through ATSA, as you know, there is a minimum compensation level that is set. That is a threshold. Above that, you have the FCE, which is the ceiling of which it would cost——

Mr. SANFORD. I understand. Why don't we do this, I would like to get in written form submitted to the committee the break-out on that front, because you have alluded to it with the Chairman, and you are alluding to me now. Let's just go, back of the envelope. You are a Federal worker, what if we just took out your retirement benefits, what would you say?

Mr. BENNER. The compensation package——

Mr. SANFORD. No, I am asking what you would say, yea or nay?

Mr. BENNER. It depends on my particular situation. In my case, you know, I have a spouse who has got a good compensation package, so I could live with the wages. I think that is kind of a flexibility actually that the contractors and vendors actually have.

Mr. SANFORD. How many real people, say, I will give up my retirement pay, not going to worry about that, my spouse will cover it, and we are not going worry about that package of dollars I would otherwise get on a yearly—how many real-world people say that?

Mr. BENNER. But that is a flexibility that the vendors—the contractors can actually have, is they can have more of a variance in terms of what they offer is pieces of their compensation package.

Mr. SANFORD. I know, but it still leaves in place the differential in a Federal worker not having accounted against them, I am getting this package of benefits and I am going to compete with the private worker who is going to—you are going have offer 401(k) plans or whatever it might be.

So it still strikes me and I would love to get in written form, because I am down to a minute and 16, a breakdown in your eyes on that, because I still don't have any arms around it. I don't think you fully explained it to the Chairman either.

Two other quick questions in my minute left, one is to the GAO: In your study of performance, it still strikes me that this, too, is an apples-and-oranges comparison. So I think we have an apples-and-oranges phenomenon with regard to compensation package that disadvantaged private vendors that you end up in 95/5 split in terms of overall distribution of folks employed.

But it still seems to me the same exists with the GAO report because if you had a start-up, which in many of these SPP programs are, and you are competing against a group of TSA workers, some of who may have been employed for 10 or more years, there would be a level of competency that would go with those years of work, and those skills acquired, and you are competing against folks who may not have as many years. So it strikes me that while you said slightly better in some cases, slightly worse than others. Did you extrapolate out the years worked within those respective populations or no?

Ms. GROVER. In the performance data, there is no controlling for the difference in the years of experience.

Mr. SANFORD. So then, I mean, most folks from a statistical standpoint would say that is not really an apples-and-apples comparison, and I see I am 15 seconds over.

You may have closing comments on that, and I thank you for the time, Mr. Chairman.

Mr. HUDSON. Ms. Grover, please feel free to answer.

Ms. GROVER. The performance data does not show overarching trends in difference in performance between SPP airports an non-SPP airports. The SPP airports were stronger in some areas, not as strong as others, but on the whole, they do seem to perform at an equivalent level regardless of the number of years of experience on the workforce.

I do think with regard to——

Mr. SANFORD. Which if I might, and, I'm over on time and will yield back, but then that would suggest to me that the private vendors were doing that much better than the GAO report even says, because you are competing with folks who, in many cases, had many more years of work experience.

With that, I yield back, Mr. Chairman.

Mr. HUDSON. Thank you.

At this time, the Chairman will recognize the gentleman from Alabama, Mr. Rogers, for any questions that he might have.

Mr. ROGERS. Ms. Grover, you talked about the comparative study. I know initially you said it was a snapshot in time, but then they accepted your recommendations to do it over a different period of time. What period of time was that subsequent review done?

Ms. GROVER. Yes, sir, the first review looked at 2012, and then the second one just came out looking at the data from 2013.

Mr. ROGERS. So you do feel like those were long-enough periods of time to get a pretty comfortable——

Ms. GROVER. Uh-huh, what TSA is doing is they are trying to look back, and they are seeing in general over this year, how did SPP airports perform as a group, compared to non-SPP airports sort-of by category.

Mr. ROGERS. How many airports had SPP presence?

Ms. GROVER. That would be 14 underway now with contracts up and running.

Mr. ROGERS. Are they all Category X airports?

Ms. GROVER. No, sir. I believe one is Category X and the rest are smaller.

Mr. ROGERS. Okay. Now, I know you talked a little while ago about folks being able to transfer over from TSA status to an SPP program. When you have that happen, and this could be for Mr. Benner, on average, how many employees choose to leave the agency and go over to the private company when that happens, when there is a transfer?

Mr. BENNER. Yes, sir, the last time we actually did that, you had a conversion from Federal to contractor, I believe was actually back in 2007. So you got to go through a span of time in order to get there.

We are in the process right now of transitioning to a number of Montana airports. There are approximately give-or-take 81 employees at four Montana airports. I don't know of the final number that are going to be—that would be transferring, but I would guess it would be around 50 percent, maybe slightly more.

Mr. ROGERS. Well, I have been on this committee for a very long time, and one of the things that we have found with TSA is a retention problem. Do we see that same retention problem by the SPP programs?

Mr. BENNER. Sir, I can't say that we do because we don't track HR, human resource kinds of functions with the SPP airports. That is one of the things that the vendor is actually responsible for, is all the HR functions, attrition, absenteeism, things like that, so we don't track that.

Mr. ROGERS. The cost of the HR function, is that calculated into your comparative of values or expenses with the two programs? The administrative portion of what it costs to have a Federal employee as opposed to just sending a check every month to a contractor?

Mr. BENNER. In the sense that when an airport goes SPP, there is a review done of that particular airport to see what support functions are being provided to that airport, and what may no longer be necessary, given now we have gone to a contract screener force.

Mr. ROGERS. Well, that is not what I am getting at. My point is this, if you have got Federal employees, like at Reagan National, that are performing the TSA function, there are some administrative expenses associated with that, other than just their pay and their benefits package. That is you have to have the infrastructure for the human resources to do the hiring, the monitoring, the evaluation, you have to have a payroll department to do that. You get my point. Were those associated costs added into the cost of having a Federal employee?

Mr. BENNER. Yeah it is included as part of the FCE, the Federal Cost Estimate. All those costs were included in there. It is up to the contractor, of course, to decide how much he or she wants to expand it.

Mr. ROGERS. I recognized the contractor, you are writing a check. That is the extent of your responsibility.

Mr. BENNER. Yes, that is correct.

Mr. ROGERS. Ms. Grover, TSA's original cost estimate stated that cost of screening was 17 percent higher at SPP airports than at non-SPP airports. Their updated 2011 estimated stated that was closer to 3 percent. More recently they have said there is barely any difference. What led to the difference in these estimates? Was it that more broad review that you did, as opposed to the snapshot in time? What accounts for that?

Ms. GROVER. Well, the cost estimate is really all driven by the assumptions that you are making. So, in the first 17 percent difference, that is when TSA was including only the costs to TSA. Then GAO came in and said, you know, we have concerns about these other costs are aren't being included. All of the Federal financial accounting standards that tell us, they tell us that whenever you are making a comparison of cost, it really needs to be a full accounting for both costs on both sides.

So TSA updated the estimate, including the total Federal cost, and as a result, the difference between the SPP and the non-SPP airports shrank to 3 percent. The current numbers—the current estimate now is essentially the costs would be about the same for this past year. But it is all driven by the assumptions that you make.

So, for example, in the most recent SPP annual report, one of the things that TSA talks about is how they recently learned that attrition in the non-SPP airports was higher. As a result, they had to increase the assumption of what their costs would be for that. So this is one of the things that we will be looking at in our study going forward and just trying to understand how reasonable those assumptions are and how they result in the cost differences and estimates.

Mr. ROGERS. Well, it appears to me that the better you get at looking at this, the more cost beneficial the SPP airports are, the more you are able to focus on where the real costs are in the Federal programs.

Thank you very much, a very good job. I appreciate you, and I yield back.

Mr. HUDSON. I thank the gentleman.

Without objection, I would like to do another round of questions if that is okay with the witnesses.

Mr. Benner, on the previous panel, Mr. VanLoh testified that during the rebid of the contract to Kansas City, TSA did not request Kansas City airport's input on the incumbent's prior performance before awarding the contract to a new private bidder. I am just curious.

He also said that TSA chose the lowest bidder, despite TSA's recently announcing pay increases for Federal screeners at other airports. Is it standard practice for TSA to not request the input the airport operator regarding the performance of incumbent screening company during a rebid contract?

Mr. BENNER. The evaluation of vendors who propose a contract— who propose to have a contract, they may submit a number of different references and they also talk about their past performance.

Certainly, we talked to the FSD. We expect the FSD, Federal Security Directors, to be talking to the airports as well to get feedback. In addition to that, we also look at various Government-wide systems to see what the history of the vendor is for potentially other contracts.

Mr. HUDSON. Is there a formal process where the FSD is tasked with communicating with airport directors— because that is the first time I have heard that.

Mr. BENNER. No, there is not. We expect the FSD's to interacting with their airport directors all the time. We expect that of all our FSDs, not just the ones that have SPP airports.

Mr. HUDSON. It just seems to me to it would inform the decision have more input from the airport operator, like the FSD is there, it just seems the more information you could have, the more transparency, the better decision that could be made on that contract. Whether it is positive or negative about the incumbent vendor, it just seems to me there ought to be more of that in this process as an observation.

Mr. Brenner and Ms. Grover, do you think it would be viable to hear from airport—do you think it would add value to have more input from airport? I guess I will ask Ms. Grover what you think, based on my comments and the question we just presented.

Ms. GROVER. I think more input is always useful.

Mr. HUDSON. Okay, gavel down, input is good.

Getting back to the question—I sort of ran through like 10 questions at you the last time. How confident are you that TSA is selecting the best value proposal when evaluating the SPP bids as opposed to simply taking the lowest bid offer?

Mr. BENNER. I am glad you put it that way, sir, because we do select the best value. That does not mean the lowest bid. There is three general criteria that we use to evaluate: There is a technical solution that the offeror provides; there is the past performance; and then there is the cost. All those three are actually evaluated.

Then you have different teams that actually evaluate each of those. Then that goes to a source selection authority, who then compares all those relative to each other and makes a final selection.

In some cases, there is even another level, a source selection evaluation board, which is in the case of—the last time we went through MCI, there was another level of observation there as well. So I am confident that we are selecting the vendor who had the best proposal overall and provides the best value to the Government. Does that mean that it won't be protested? Absolutely not. Because any vendor can obviously protest it, any time if they feel they have been wronged or the process has been wronged, but I am confident in the process that we use.

Mr. HUDSON. Well, I don't want to inject myself into any specific case or especially one that is in the courts now, but an example of Kansas City, hearing the airport director talk about the fact they have folks who have been there may be 12 years now, have a lot of experience whose compensation is probably reflecting that. Then you have got the standard that requires what the minimum level pay is. If you bring in a new vendor—and I will say hypothetically, let's not talk about Kansas City specifically—but if you were to bring in a new vendor at that minimum pay level, TSA pay level, they couldn't afford to retain these experienced workers that worked in these same checkpoints who have this better experience. So, even if you are selecting a new vendor, with all this information, you are sort of precluding your best screeners from being able to continue to be employed there by a different vendor.

I think on one hand, I am not sure we are taking into account that experience level of that vendor. We kind-of addressed that, but even if you then decide there is better value of a new vendor, I have concerns that these minimum standards mean we are not even going to be able to keep our best screeners. There are sort of two questions here that as I heard the testimony today and really concern me. I don't know if you would like to address that or——

Mr. BENNER. Well, again, I want to be clear on the ATSA minimum that we actually set is actually the Federal equivalent plus the locality pay. So that is a fairly robust minimum. But you are absolutely correct, Mr. Chairman, that the difference between that number there and the FCE at the very top gives the vendor the latitude to design the compensation package that he or she feels is best to run the screening operation of that particular airport.

Now, on the flip side, if we were to require everybody to get the exact same amount of pay that they had gotten, say, in their previous job, whether they were Federal or whether they were contractor, we have now moved the floor and the ceiling so close together, if you will, that there would be many vendors that could probably not compete or wouldn't want to compete because the profit margin just wouldn't be there.

Mr. HUDSON. I certainly understand that. That is kind-of my concern. If you continue to look at it this way, I don't see how an experienced vendor could ever get reissued their contract because you are always going to have incentive for the new vendor to always undershoot the number, and all they have to do is hire an inexperienced staff and pay them lower to win that contract.

It seems to me it would make more sense to have an average to give flexibility to the vendors so they can make decisions about how they are going to meet the cost rather than setting this minimum floor that, again, is going to make it—I don't see how any existing vendor is going to be able get renewed if they have got someone willing to come in and undershoot them. It seems we ought to be looking at averages, maybe, instead of system as you described it.

Mr. BENNER. Sir, if I may, I am afraid I am maybe not being clear in how I am articulating this.

Mr. HUDSON. I may be slow in hearing what you are saying.

Mr. BENNER. I doubt that. I doubt that. So the FCE, the Federal Cost Estimate, is actually based on the actual. So, in other words, the entire pay that everybody is getting at that particular airport, whether it is an SPP or it is Federal, is actually taken into that Federal Cost Estimate. That becomes the ceiling. So, theoretically, that vendor has the latitude to pay all the way up to that. So they could hypothetically be paid——

Mr. HUDSON. But if they are trying to win a bid, they are going to go as low as possible in order to get the business, and so there is an incentive then to have—so if you are not taking into account this bidding process the experience of the current vendor, the input of the airport director of the quality of that vendor, then I could start a fly-by-night company and go in there and underbid and get the contract, but I wouldn't be able to afford to pay any experienced screeners. So I am just afraid there is a perverse incentive set-up that penalizes you for being experienced and having good employees you have retained, but it is an incentive for any upstart company to come in and undershoot that. Again, I am not talking any airport specifically. It is just that these issues made me question the overall process.

Mr. BENNER. May I respond?

Mr. HUDSON. Sure, please.

Mr. BENNER. So that would be I think entirely true, if in, in fact, it was based only on low price. But you also in the evaluation process have a technical proposal that needs to be provided by a vendor, as well as past performance. So it doesn't mean strictly someone who submits the low bid automatically wins the contract.

Mr. HUDSON. I certainly appreciate that. I would love to have more discussions with you sort-of about the input from when we do these—reissue these contracts and making sure we are getting input from the airport directors and all sources. I think my approach with Government is the more sunlight, the more input, the more discussion, the better decisions are made.

I appreciate the time you have taken today to answer our questions. I would ask that both of you be willing to respond in writing to any questions the committee may want to submit. I want to continue this discussion, because again, I do believe in this program. I do believe private screening is more efficient. I think it can be more effective. I think it is where we need to go in the future as we try to deal with continued threats in aviation security, as we try to address those, giving the best deal to the taxpayers, best security to the American people.

I believe the strength of this program is important. I want to see it grow, but I want to work with you to make sure there aren't structural concerns. I want to make sure there aren't biases within TSA against this program. I think it is an important component in our overall safety footprint. So it is an issue that is very important to me and something I think we need it continue to talk about and continue to work on. But I thank both of you for being here today and your testimony in this.

So, with that, the subcommittee stands adjourned.

[Whereupon, at 11:15 a.m., the subcommittee was adjourned.]

○

www.ingramcontent.com/pod-product-compliance
Lightning Source LLC
Chambersburg PA
CBHW080518290526
45790CB00006B/2225